By Hook and By Crook

FRED ARCHER

LARGE PRINT
Oxford

Copyright © Fred Archer, 1978

First published in Great Britain 1978
by
Hodder and Stoughton Ltd

Published in Large Print 2004 by ISIS Publishing Ltd,
7 Centremead, Osney Mead, Oxford OX2 0ES
by arrangement with
The Estate of Fred Archer

The moral right of the author has been asserted

British Library Cataloguing in Publication Data
Archer, Fred, 1915–
    By hook and by crook. – Large print ed. –
    (Isis reminiscence series)
    1. Farm life – England – Worcestershire – History
    – 19th century
    2. Large type books
    3. Evesham, Vale of (England) – Social life and
    customs – 19th century
    I. Title
    942.4'49081

ISBN 0–7531–9962–9 (hb)
ISBN 0–7531–9963–7 (pb)

Printed and bound by Antony Rowe, Chippenham

Contents

To my good friend and editor
Margaret Body

CHAPTER
ONE

Carrants Field

A winding brook, slow-flowing through the meadows under Bredon Hill, is a thing of little consequence except that the old land drains empty the brown earth-stained water at intervals along its course. Carrants Brook is its name — a name derived from the owner of the land in the Middle Ages — Alexander Karante. I wonder what sort of a man Alexander was? Perhaps he cleared the stream of fallen withy or willow trees or conserved the eels, trout and watercress for his table. There is a lot more to Carrants Brook than the distant recall of Alexander.

Carrants Field lies on the eastern side of the water and when the giant carve-up of enclosure was made in 1773 the brook was a dividing line. The Parish of Ashton, where earlier fields were mounded or fenced on Bredon Hill, had nine hundred and twenty acres of land enclosed by the Parliamentary Award. Lord Tyrconnel received three hundred and fifty-two acres for his land and tithes. The vicar seventy-nine acres for his tithes. Henry Wakeman, squire of neighbouring Beckford, one hundred and ten acres for land and tithes, and the Deacle Charity, eighty acres. Two other

1

proprietors had over thirty acres, while thirteen Ashton men staked their claim and had allotments varying from a quarter of an acre to eleven acres. This was Carrants Field.

The parish itself was an area much larger than nine hundred and twenty acres, but the Baldwyn family who had been here for five hundred years farmed the lower slopes of Bredon and grazed that plateau of over nine hundred feet with cattle and sheep. Enclosure had been no more ruthless here than in other parishes and it's heartening to know that thirteen labourers were able to keep an allotment although they lost the right to graze common land on Bredon because the common was fenced.

Henry Jephcott, a lawyer from Northampton, stayed at the Red Lion at Beckford to do the official business. He had other legal men with him to settle disputes. An Ashton labourer, who was dispossessed of his strip of arable, murdered Jephcott but he was never hanged at Gloucester Castle.

You may well wonder why my interest lies in Carrants Field.

Thomas and Elizabeth Archer came to Ashton in 1800 from Dumbleton. Thomas was a carpenter who inherited an allotment in Carrants Field when his father William died on October 18th, 1827. William had two other sons, George, and young William, born in the year his father died. It was this William who was my grandfather. So it happened that way back in the reign of George IV my great grandfather grew his acre of wheat, his potatoes and beans in Carrants Field alongside the brook, nearly a hundred years before the railway cut the land of the labourers in two parts to make their line.

Thomas Archer was no scholar, but in 1814 about thirty young folk were having some sort of schooling. I still have one of his bills for work done to a house in Ashton in 1814.

	£	s.	d.
Oak Lining for wall plate		1	6
Pair of door hinges			6
Hand rail		1	0
80′ of 1″ board at 3½d.	1	8	4
Labour 40 days at 3d.	6	0	0
Paling for Pig Ousen (house)			9

William Archer, my grandfather, as I said, first saw the light of day in 1827 when George IV was doing his short stint as King of England. Wondering and searching, as I do, to recapture life here under Bredon Hill, the year William's father died and he was born, Great Uncle Thomas, who lived to the ripe old age of ninety-seven, remembered as a boy the enclosure of the village and told my Uncle Jim all about it, how his dad lost the grazing on Bredon Hill, but was allowed four acres in Carrants Field.

Thomas told Uncle Jim that regardless of the feudal system he was a Tory, wore a bit of blue ribbon in his hat and gave Uncle a humbug from a tin on the mantel

3

shelf when young Jimmy said, "I'm a Tory, Uncle. I'll vote for them one day."

Now Grandfather was Liberal and Chapel, and later on was to join the Methodists when they met in Garrets cottage. As a boy he drove a team of horses to plough. He never went to school and could neither read nor write. Uncle Jim said that once in 1822, when he was doing a job for Squire Baldwyn, his Uncle Thomas, the carpenter, saw William Cobbett on Bredon Hill.

Cobbett describes life in Gloucestershire at that time. So much better than Wiltshire, he says. "The Gloucestershire people have no notion of dying with hunger. No worn features. There is a pig in every sty. Their cultivated gardens grow apple trees. Most of the year they have apple puddings and the strips of land are let to the labourers at £1 per acre to grow potatoes, wheat and greens."

It's good to think that here between the Cotswolds and the Malverns, cider, fat bacon and dumplings probably made life not much poorer after enclosure. So, as Great Uncle Thomas was hanging a gate for Squire Baldwyn and Great Grandfather was ploughing the limestone hill with a bullock team, they never knew that the man they met would go down in history as he has done.

Cobbett, writing of Wiltshire, found the land neglected. He says he could plant sainfoin, clover and rye grass after turnips and keep feeding off with sheep until the sainfoin and clover take over. But he did like the houses, the yards, the trees and the rookeries. He counted twenty-two ricks in one yard; four thousand sheep in one fold. He writes however, that the wages at 6d. per week didn't please him as the men who grew the corn and produced the beef were living on potatoes.

Cobbett rode from Upton-on-Severn, famous for Fielding and Tom Jones, through Strensham, the Samuel Butler country, to Squire Hanford's house at Woolass Hall. His estate, Cobbett records, is one of the highest in the county. It adjoins Ashton Parish and the Parish Quarry.

Cobbett, that great radical, was for ever having a dig at the idle rich and the clergy, but my feeling is he must have had means to travel himself, accompanied by his manservant and well-mounted on horseflesh through many counties.

From the summit of Bredon, he says, ten counties can be seen. The Vale of Evesham, Worcester and Gloucester having the rivers Avon and Severn winding down towards the Bristol Channel. Certainly you see from Bredon Hill one of the richest spots in England. "Richer than any in the world except Scotland." These are Cobbett's words, and who am I to argue with him?

"The finest meadows some one hundred acres." Here he must be referring to the Great Ham or River Meadow at Twyning. "Nine tenths of the land is pasture grazed by Hereford cattle and Leicester sheep." Was Cobbett an authority on sheep? Surely the sheep would be Cotswold — quite similar to the Leicester.

At Squire Hanford's at Woolass Hall on Bredon slopes he mentions the Roman Catholic chapel high up in the roof, twenty-five foot by ten. It has an arch to imitate the roof of a church and a priest hole with a trap door through which English gentlemen, who remained faithful to the Roman Church, could escape the hands of James I's Calvinistic Scottish followers. Cobbett hadn't a good word to say for them, but plenty instead for "that honest Englishman" Guy Fawkes who wished to blow the Scots back to their mountains. In the Hall Cobbett saw a portrait of one of the Gunpowder plotters, Sir Thomas Winter, who hid there but was caught and killed by the sheriff.

Of Colonel Hastings Davies who had recently come to neighbouring Elmley Castle, he speaks with great affection. "As M.P. for Worcester may he show his mettle." Alas, his chance to do so was short-lived. The Colonel bought Elmley Park in 1822 but while he was canvassing in Worcester for an election of 1834 he was thrown from his carriage by hooligans and injured so badly he became paralysed. Tragedy for a man who had fought at Waterloo, for he died soon after the attack in the City of Worcester. Thomas Archer, the carpenter, remembered the death of Colonel Davies and in his old age passed the record on to Uncle Jim Archer. Indeed, Thomas remembered the whole military family from Elmley, but Colonel Hastings Davies, a godson of Warren Hastings, was mourned all around Bredon Hill.

Looking at the riches of the land around Bredon, Cobbett made one other remark with which it would have been hard to disagree. "It's odd," he said, "that in so fertile a spot, how the roads have been neglected."

CHAPTER
TWO

Down Dewrest Lane

Ashton parish is in the hundred or district of Tibblestone. The stone stands as it did in Thomas Archer's time at the Tewkesbury to London turnpike at Teddington.

Teddington Hands is a landmark — a finger post of wooden fingers on a stone pillar pointing to seven towns and villages. I'm sure Thomas Archer in his travels with the carpenter's tools must have read the words beneath the hands.

> Edmund Attwood of The Vine Tree
> At the first erected me
> And freely he did this bestow
> Strange travellers the way to show
> To eight generations past and gone
> Repaired by Alice Attwood of Teddington.

Before 1812 the main road here was from Tewkesbury to Stow-on-the-Wold and London. Cheltenham had not grown to much importance, so the crossing to Evesham was a rutted track while the road to Cheltenham was through Winchcombe.

The Vale of Evesham Road Club was formed just before the nineteenth century dawned. The landowners were ashamed of the state of the roads. The Club wrote to the Quarter Sessions at Worcester as follows:

"Bad roads are the only blemish and disgrace to our County. A County happy beyond every other in its situation, soil, variety and plenty of produce."

The village squires met at the Angel at Pershore, the Swan at Tewkesbury, the Crown at Evesham and the White Hart at Winchcombe, every month at two-thirty. They had dinner for half a crown, with a further half a crown for liquor — the five-shilling bill to be called at six o'clock. Districts were planned, surveyors appointed, and soon Umberlands Lane and Dewrest Lane from Hinton on the Green to Teddington Hands was made a road fit for the traffic of the day.

Before the Club took over, the London road to Tewkesbury from Hinton on the Green went over Bredon Hill, a steep and cumbersome journey through the woods, the rabbit warrens, the quarries, dropping down into the Vale at Overbury. No wonder a landlord was waylaid in a coppice on Bredon slopes and murdered, while his assailant took his bag of rent money he had collected from farmers in the hill villages. An unkind place at night was the old London Road. I would think it was an old drovers' road, one of the many green lanes which the cattle and sheep men used on their way to Smithfield Market.

Who were the public spirited men of the Vale? James Martin, Squire of Overbury, William Wakeman of Beckford, Squire Baldwyn of Ashton, Thomas Attwood of Teddington and John Parsons, Squire of Kemerton, who built for his pleasure, Parsons Folly, that tower 1,000 feet up on Bredon summit.

When the rules were drawn up they were posted on church doors and in markets. In Ashton, David Drinkwater of the Orchard Farm was appointed surveyor, while the work was done in the parish by George Archer, Thomas's other brother, and Job Barnett. These two men quarried the limestone off Bredon to make good Umberlands Lane, while David Drinkwater hauled the loaded carts.

"We be mending our ways," George and Job said as they drank their cider in the Star Inn.

It's amazing how men of little education can work to a nicety with stone or wood. What is known as the scowl of brow method — measurements obtained and levels done without spirit levels, just a look and a pace or two and the job is there, under the billy cock hat of what some would call country yokels. Not since the Romans built the Salt Way through the village, had a scheme of road making and improving been done here. The surveyors told Job, George and the men from the other villages to make the surface dead level, but rounded to verge trenches to carry away the water along Umberlands Lane and Dewrest Lane.

Foundations were made of hedge croppings, furze or twigs lying crossways on the road, then large stones were laid at the bottom, decreasing to gravel at the top. Every stone had to be weathered, exposed to the air for twelve months so that Job and George's stacks of stone were not hauled away from the Parish Quarry for a year. The surveyor called new stone soft and green.

The idea of a foundation of twigs is very old, for long before tile drains were laid in the field to take the water, trenches were dug and filled with faggots of ash twigs tied in bundles with a withy twig, then the top soil replaced. These primitive drains worked well in the stiff clay of the Midland plain, forming an underground drain which lasted for years.

The Turnpike Act declared that no waggon or four-wheeled carriage should be pulled by more than three horses, ensuring that the new road would not be rutted by too heavy traffic. The wheels or felloes, should be at least six inches wide. This seemed fair enough for farm waggons and carts, but I imagine some passenger vehicles would be hit by this rule. The owner of a waggon who broke the law was to be fined £5 and the driver twenty shillings. It was David Drinkwater, the surveyor, who saw twenty horses pulling a waggon up Broadway Hill in a snowstorm. The road there was steep and bad, and it didn't come under the Evesham Road Club.

In his lean-to, full of tools and timber, Thomas Archer, the carpenter, worked with his saws, his draw shave, his spoke shave. With the road-building under way along the Dewrest and Umberlands Lane, the Evesham Road Club had got him busy making wheelbarrows to wheel the Bredon Hill stone for the road-making.

His younger brother, George, became assistant to David Drinkwater.

"Who is paying for all this yer caper, making roads as level and easy to walk on like Parson Timbrell's drive?" George asked. "I'll allow I get my twelve or fourteen bob a week, Master Drinkwater sees to that. Somebody pays him no doubt. Got a fine horse and cart, he has, and his Missus got a piano, 'cos I've been to Orchard Farm."

David Drinkwater explained to Thomas and George how each village was responsible for its own roads and supplied the materials and the labour. The money for this came from the ratepayers of the village, the rates being fixed at the Vestry Meeting. Thomas Archer knew now that the Parish Clerk would pay him for the wheelbarrows.

"We need some means of firming the road surface," David spoke to Thomas in his workshop one morning. The carts and waggons and carriages of the day had such narrow wheels that the road was constantly being rutted.

Thomas replied, "I suppose you have some sort of roller in mind, David." And when the surveyor agreed, the carpenter replied in a jocular way, "Any perry pears on your trees this year at the orchard?"

"Yes," came David Drinkwater's answer, "but why do you ask?"

"'Tis like this, David. I made a useful roller to roll Master Baldwyn's wheat at the Manor from the trunk of a perry pear tree. Nothing makes a roller so well as a pear tree butt."

"All right, then, when the fruit is shaken and picked up for cider and perry in my orchard, you can cut a suitable tree down and make me a roller." David was a little reluctant to sacrifice one of his Malvern Hill perry pear trees, but was anxious to make a good job of the remade turnpike road, Dewrest Lane.

"I'll want a hand to fell and trim a tree of that size," Thomas explained to David that he would also need Squire Baldwyn's timber waggon and a team of horses to move the tree trunk down Cottons Lane to his yard and workshop.

"Take your brother George to help and no doubt Mr. Baldwyn will let young William come along too."

It was Christmas before the fruit in Drinkwater's orchard had been gathered for cider and perry and crushed at the mill at nearby Bumbo. On New Year's Day when the overnight frost had knitted the ground together to make the travelling so much easier for horses and for men, Thomas Archer took some tools up to Drinkwater's farm orchard where he met his brother, George. Together they sawed and axed the tree. Thomas sent his younger brother up among the branches with a waggon rope. When the saw and the axes had nearly cut through the reddish-brown pear wood, the brother pulled on the rope. The timber creaked as it swayed.

"He's talking a bit, George, now for a good pull," and with this the tree fell in a gap among the fruit trees belonging to David Drinkwater who stood at his back door with a jar of cider.

"When do you need the waggon, men?" he said.

"After dinner when we have shudded the tree of its branches," Thomas replied. As they sat together, the brothers and David on the tree trunk, Thomas explained to the other two men how he would make the roller. The trunk was nearly two feet in diameter and fifteen feet long. Thomas aimed to make a roller nine feet six wide so that it would go in between the ten feet gates in the village fields. In fact it was the same design as the one he made for Squire Henry Baldwyn.

Alf Stubbs and William Archer arrived on the scene after dinner with the timber waggon pulled by three of the Squire's horses.

"Now, I've done a bit of timber loading, Alf, so show me your most reliable horse."

"Oi, Turpin, he can pull and I've brought along a roller chain on purpose to load tree, 'cos we load a few every winter and take them to Master Baldwyn's saw pit."

Turpin in traces pulled the trunk up the two skid poles placed alongside the waggon until the tree was in position ready to be taken to Thomas's workshop. At the workshop, when the tree had been unloaded, David Drinkwater gave orders for Thomas's brother George to help with the making of the roller.

"February Fill Dyke," the surveyor said. "That's the time to roll in the stones and the soil and the sand to make the road. When it rains most days, that 'ull bind the surface."

Then Thomas spoke up in the shop. "Get that peeling iron, the one I use to peel the oak trees, George boy, and split the bark lengthways on opposite sides of the trunk with this here hatchet, then use the peeling iron to peel off the bark."

George got busy on his brother's instructions, peeling the trunk, while Thomas began to bore a hole from one end to receive the iron axles. "Nine foot six I said, didn't I? Ah, now we'll get the cross cut saw and cut the trunk to that length."

The pear tree now with all the little knots and bulges cut off was as straight and as round as the barrel of a cannon. Thomas Archer, with the help of his brother, then made a framework of four-inch by two-inch wood to fix to the axle and to take the shafts for the horse.

In all Thomas's years as wheelwright he had worked closely with the village blacksmith, Herbert Butler. It was important to co-operate when wheels were to be tyred and on other joint jobs with farm and road vehicles. Herbert came along at Thomas Archer's request to size up the iron work for the roller. He measured carefully with his rule, then, back at the forge, he shaped in white hot iron two bearings which bolted on to the wooden frame and reached down to the axle. At each end of the axle the crude iron bearings were formed, like large washers, to receive the round axle. This fitted fairly tightly with enough room for some axle grease to be daubed on the axle.

Where the axle came through the bearings, a split had been forged in the metal to receive a split pin to prevent the roller from coming out of the frame. Two iron ferrules hammered on each end of the trunk to prevent the wood from splitting were the only other jobs Hubert Butler did on the making of the roller, apart, that is, from making the hooks and staples and ridge chain for the shafts, but Thomas fixed these items. The shafts Thomas made from two straight ash poles from Ashton Wood, seasoned they were and had hung overhead in his shop for some years.

When the roller was finished, George Archer took it down Gypsies Lane, over the Carrant Brook Bridge to the new Cheltenham Road, or shall we say, the reconstructed road. With two of Squire Baldwyn's horses, Sharper as filler, or shaft horse, and Turpin in chains as trace horse, the new roller bounced and bumped over the rough surface of that old bit of Roman Saltway.

David Drinkwater was anxious to see how the roller pushed the little stones and gravel into place to make a reasonable surface. The men working there with their stone hammers, shovels, pickaxes and rammers, stood back while Great Uncle George led his two horses along a stretch of roadway.

"Thur now," the men said, "that 'ull save us a smart bit of ramming with the iron rammer, look ya. Thomas's roller makes a tidy job of levelling."

Tons upon tons of Bredon Hill stone were rolled into that road. Bredon Hill stone wasn't as hard as the stuff from Clee Hill. Job Barnett and his men worked long hours at the Parish Quarry eight hundred feet up on the hill. Alf Stubbs hauled the stone weeks on end in cart loads from the workings past the beech trees in sight of Parsons Folly. The Squire, knowing the need, sent loads of stones the women picked up in the corn fields. They carried them in their aprons of hurden and stacked them in little heaps for the men to load in the carts. It was almost like an orchestra beating time when the workmen's hammers were cracking the limestone. Every stone had to be split down the grain, like wood, and after the heavy sledge hammers had made them smaller, the men used the little stone hammers with nut stick handles to crack the lumps to size as they wedged them beneath their hobnailed boots.

Fred Dunn and Jim Dance, Squire Baldwyn's groom, agreed that the sooner the road-making was finished the better. "All we hear in the Star these nights is talk from Umberlands Lane. 'How many yards did we lay today, George?' 'Master Drinkwater paid me fifteen shilling a Saturday.'"

"I be mortal sick to year of road-makers and the noise of their hammers," Fred said to Jim.

"Thee just wait and see, Fred Dunn, 'cos when this yer main road a got a face on Master Drinkwater told me as he ull be no more than an hour with his hoss and cyart gwain to Cheltenham," George boasted.

"'Tis a sadding din, day after day, the tip-tapping of the roadman's hammers." It was clear from his tone Fred would be pleased to see George and his fellow workers back working on the land with him where they belonged.

"We be as far as Beckford Inn and now keeps our eyes cocked Tibblestone way, looking for the tother gang working this a road," was George's comment when Fred chaffed him about the slowness of roadmaking.

The Parish Clerk meanwhile reported the progress of the Ashton roadmen at the Vestry Meeting in St. Barbara's Church. The Umberlands Lane section was nearly finished. Archdeacon Timbrell said that he personally was glad to hear the sound of hammers working and looked forward to having a decent road for his coach and pair to take him around other parishes in the diocese.

So the road was completed from Ashton turnpike to the Tibblestone.

CHAPTER
THREE

Ash Stick and Holly Wood

It's true that every alteration to established farming practice has always been viewed with suspicion, and sometimes with hostility, by the farm labourer.

No doubt there was some opposition to Jethro Tull's invention of the corn drill, for hadn't man sown the seed from a straw skep or similar basket from time immemorial? Was it the fear of men being unemployed, or was it a genuine concern that seed sown in drills, rather than broadcast, would not yield as good a crop at harvest? I would say it's a mixture of the two, but there is another factor that is a die-hard belief in farm workers, that if anything new is tried out on the land in cultivation, planting, harvest and threshing, and that practice makes the work easier, it must be wrong. There is in every farming man a sense almost of sanctity in sheer hard work. Adam was told in Eden that by the sweat of his brow he would eat bread, and easier ways are frowned upon.

My grandfather was too young to remember the troubles of 1830, but his elder brother Thomas, the carpenter, remembered and told Uncle Jim about the hard life that sparked them off. Over at Beckford Hall Farm, for example, Martin and Jim Allen were stone-picking in September at a little over a shilling a day. In October when the men had cleared the stubbles of the stooks of wheat, Jim and Martin breast ploughed the land to clean the top soil of weeds. Eight shillings per acre was the rate for this job. A job where the breast plough blade is set at an angle from the long handle, which is pushed by the thighs of the ploughmen who wear wooden boards on top of their cord trousers, boards fastened to the front of their thighs by leather thongs of raw hide. To plough two or three inches deep on good soil is still hard work.

Sudden deaths were always to remain a mystery in the early nineteenth century, but one breast ploughman, Felix Culshaw, died, it's stated, from affection of the heart. Isaac Salisbury was present at his death. I suppose he had heart failure, but affection of the heart would affect the love life of a ploughman as much as a Squire. To push the breast plough over an eight-acre field would, I imagine, break many a heart.

In Worcestershire in 1830 a married man was preferred to a single man on the land because parish relief for his children saved the employer's wages. There was an even better source of income, according to Henderson's *Village Labourer* — marrying the mother of bastards. Bastards were more profitable, since the parish guaranteed the contribution for which the father should have been liable. One young woman of twenty-four with four bastard children put it this way.

19

"If I had one more, I would be comfortable." So women with bastard children were very eligible wives for labourers.

The revolt of the labourers in 1830 was a backlash of Enclosure. One man said his father had eaten meat, bacon, cheese and vegetables when he had his strip of land, and now he, the son, was reduced to potatoes and bread, and ceased to brew any beer. Some lived on roots, swedes and sorrel and drank tea kettle broth instead of tea. Tea kettle broth is made from hot water poured on burnt toast with salt and pepper.

When the first threshing machines were introduced in Britain so soon after Enclosure, the village labourer understandably protested. His whole winter had been spent in the barns on the threshing floors earning his wages. The labourer still had a grudge against the Enclosures because he had lost his strip of arable and the common grazing rights, but Enclosure had increased the corn yield, so he was recompensed by an increase in his wages for threshing. A farmer who threshed all his corn with the flail might have twenty-three barns in a parish, enough work for fifteen men from harvest until May at fifteen shillings per week, piecework, and seventy-five people would benefit. The new threshing machine was a real threat to their livelihood.

On August 28th, 1830, four hundred men destroyed the threshing machines which had come into a village. The penalty was seven years' transportation. Penal law was as varied then as at any time, for where a man got seven years transportation for destroying a threshing machine, the penalty for firing a rick was the death sentence.

Uncle Jim told me how Thomas Archer, the carpenter, spoke of the Tolpuddle Martyrs of 1834, how George Loveless and his friends had new shackles riveted round their arms and legs and were sent as convicts to Australia in the ship *William Metcalf* for trying to improve their lot in Dorset, where the wage was eight shillings per week. He also remembered the transportation of villagers to Van Diemen's Land. We have a field of that name in our village. I wonder who went — and came back. Between 1788 and 1867 137,000 men were sent to Tasmania.

Although threshing machines were becoming fairly common by 1830 onwards, in the villages under Bredon Hill corn was still threshed by the flail or two stick method. No doubt some alteration in the making of this primitive implement had taken place over the years from Biblical times, but it had been for centuries an ash stick with another shorter hand stick of holly wood attached, called the swingel. This was often attached with a piece of the skin of an eel, but sometimes a leather thong hinged the two sticks together. The thresher held the long ash stick and swung it above his head, then with an aimed blow, he hit the ear of the open sheaves of corn with the short holly stick. The threshing floor was a wooden, slightly raised platform between the opposite double doors, each side of the barn. The same floor was used for sheep-shearing in June.

Squire Baldwyn's men whacked at the open sheaf with their flails, keeping a constant rhythm of the threshers' art, as each holly stick hit the floor in turn and sent up a fog of dust from the ears of corn, dust which settled on the cobwebbed timbers under the thatch, until each cobweb looked like a sleeping bat. The cider jar caught the weak rays of the winter sunshine and stood out like a giant horn lantern in the doorway.

"Thirsty work," Alf said. "After a middling wet harvest, the dust do fly from the years on the sheaves, and it makes my throat as dry as a nun's tit."

Fred cleared his throat as he poured out some cider into two small cider horns. Cider, amber, with a tinge of green and not quite claret clear, now a year old.

"Alf," Fred said, "don't ever thee let Master Timbrell, the parson, hear ya talk like that. Chairman of the Sessions, ya know, and he would have ya in front of the bench for using vulgar words."

When the grain and chaff was swept into a heap ready for the winnowing, the threshing floor shone polished like a ball room; polished and shining from hours, days, weeks, years of the whack of the flail.

The two men had no need to fear that Squire Baldwyn would buy a machine to displace them at their work. The Squire was comfortably off after the Napoleonic wars had kept the corn prices high. He was a good employer of labour and kept his men in work when they were past doing a good day's labour in the field. They still came, some on two sticks, and cropped the hawthorn hedges or cleaned out a ditch.

22

The cider in the adjoining barn was for the men and boys. A gallon a day each for threshing. While the cowman, carter and shepherd, who had to work on Sundays, were given a breakfast of bread from his oven in the great kitchen and boiled fat bacon, yellow and mature, cut from one of the flitches in the bacon rack by Jim Dance, the Squire's groom, who lived in the harness room next to the hunting stable. The men then took home cans of skim milk for their wives and children.

The chief men on the threshing floors of Ashton and Beckford were Fred Dunn and Alf Stubbs, working on Squire Baldwyn's farm, and Martin and Jim Allen who worked for George Bass, a tenant on Wakeman's estate. At the Beckford Vestry Meeting, the Allen brothers were appointed village constables for a year and at Ashton Vestry Meeting, Alf Stubbs was appointed constable. Being from neighbouring villages, the constables worked together, meeting at Grafton crossroads on duty.

"There's talk of a policeman being stationed at Beckford," Jim Allen told Alf Stubbs.

"No need for he, we allus have managed, ain't us Martin?" Alf replied as they stood together under the stone wall where the road leads to Grafton hamlet. The only recent disturbance in Ashton had been a drunken sailor who had given Archdeacon Timbrell, on the bench, a piece of his mind and ended up doing a month on the treadmill at Northleach Jail. "That's damned hard labour, mind," said Alf.

"A sight harder than swinging the threshing flail all day," Martin agreed.

Jim Allen, the older of the brothers, then described how a while back the labourers of the Beckford area met at the inn to ask for more wages because of the high price of provisions.

"There wasn't many there," he said, "but Master Timbrell sent me and Martin along in case there was trouble. Oh, Spider Watchet was there, but he's a single man without a wife to keep, and being cowman at the Hall, his job is safe enough."

"Yes, I was asked to go," Alf Stubbs said in a superior sort of tone. "I told Spider I got a missus and family to keep and Mr. Baldwyn allows me some tater ground. You know he's a good gaffer, Jim, letting me have a pig in the sty and our apple tree keeps us in apple puddings half the year, and the garden grows cabbage and beans. Don't thee upset Squire Baldwyn."

"I allus reckons to hold the candle a bit to the gentry," was Martin's comment.

"What sort of a gaffer is George Bass, Jim?" asked Alf.

"All right, you, as long as he don't go on persuading Squire Wakeman to buy that threshing tackle that bin on show at Gloucester."

Martin Allen then told Alf Stubbs what his and Jim's reaction would be as constables if threshing tackle was broken up in their village, as had happened in Oxfordshire. "Jim and me as constables 'ull be inclined to turn a blind eye if this happens, 'cos we know the feeling in the parish."

Alf Stubbs talked with Spider Watchet and Thomas Archer in the Star.

"What be I to do, Thomas, if threshing machines come to Ashton and some of the younger chaps in the village damage them?"

Thomas looked hard and thoughtful at the two young men and remembered Enclosure and a similar situation and what Great Grandfather William Archer had told him, a father-to-son confidence which, up until now, had not been broken. "At the time when the land was enclosed," he began, "Fred Dunn's father had a strip of corn ground anant our Dad's and kept a cow on the common around Holcombe Nap. Abel Dunn lost both his land and, of course, his grazing, because Holcombe Nap was enclosed and belonged to Mr. Wakeman. Dad reckoned he came off so bad on account of the fencing of Beckfords Way, the land anant his strip. He refused to pay his whack towards it so the overseers paid him out and he lost his rights."

"What did Abel Dunn do then, Thomas?" Spider asked.

"I don't want to overrun my tale, but according to father he walked these roads like a madman and took to the drink in a terrible way, he did. A tempestuous temper Abel had, not like Fred."

"Go on, Thomas, be us gwain to be yer all night, happen?" Spider called for the landlord to fill the tots up with his best beer.

"Well, you'll have heard tell of Henry Jephcott, likely — the lawyer who came here from Northampton to settle the parish award. Henry Jephcott was murdered.

By a person or persons unknown was the verdict at the coroner's inquest. But do you want to know what really happened nigh on sixty years ago?"

"If it's the truth, Thomas, let's have it," Alf said.

"Long Fred's father was constable at the time, so that's where you come in, Alf. A dutiful man, our Dad said, but he knew who murdered Henry Jephcott, and so did our Dad. Abel Dunn shot him with his flintlock. He waylaid him in the larch plantation behind the Red Lion at Beckford as he walked with his horse lantern to Beckford inn. Missing he was for some time. No one knew where the body was but Abel had put it in a couple of wheat sacks, weighed them with stone, and they found 'un in Ashton moat pond."

"Is that why Fred Dunn 'ull never go by that pond at night?" Spider asked Thomas.

"Maybe, but that's the truth and the truth needs no study. No one gave Abel away. He worked for Squire Henry until his death, but it shows you, Alf, that thurs ways and means of not always telling tales about your neighbour even if you are appointed by the Vestry as a constable."

CHAPTER
FOUR

Making Firewood of Progress

The week after Thomas Archer had told his story of the murder of Henry Jephcott there were rumours in Beckford of a threshing machine coming to the village to work on the Wakeman estate. Sam Tombs, bailiff to Squire Henry Wakeman, tried to explain to his master the obvious danger of incensing his workmen. But George Bass, the tenant of one of the farms, was a progressive man who had been urging the Squire to buying a threshing machine for a long time and George Bass prevailed. So it was that almost sixty years after the Beckford and Ashton-under-Hill Enclosure award, fresh trouble came to the villages under the Hill and a new change in the pattern of farming began to make itself felt.

Martin and Jim Allen, the constables of Beckford, had threshed George Bass's corn every winter since they were able to swing the two sticks, starting work in the big tithe barn as soon as the harvest was in. From the Michaelmas harvest morn until April, Martin and Jim had done little else, except a week or so in

November, when they worked the cider mill and pressed the apples filling George Bass's hogshead casks with the juice that would give heart to man, woman and boy for twelve months.

As Henry Wakeman's bailiff supervised the setting up of the new threshing machine in Bass's rickyard. Martin and Jim looked on with dismay. "Our livin's gwain to suffer," Martin said to his younger brother.

Jim raised his eyebrows, and answered, "We'll be on the Parish for the bit of relief."

The machine was primitive compared with the steam-propelled threshers of later years. The motive power was a horse. The horse was led in a circle by a boy. As the horse went round and round, like a cider mill, it turned a large cog wheel which was axled on the rickyard floor. This cog wheel was geared to a small cog, a shaft which turned the beaters in the threshing box.

As Wakeman's men cut the straw bands on the sheaves from the rick, another man fed the machine with the corn in the ear. The grain and chaff fell together while the straw was pushed by the shakers at the back, on to the yard floor to be tied into boltings or bundles by another two men. Nothing new about the tying of straw, for this was one of the jobs of the flail threshers. Martin and Jim tied the straw.

The grain and chaff were winnowed by another hand-turned machine called a winnower. This has a revolving fan which parts the light chaff from the corn and blows it into a heap. In a few days a whole rick of corn had been threshed which would have taken the Allen brothers weeks to do with the flail.

"No work, I'll warrant, after November," Martin forecast. "This damnable contraption 'ull be our undoing."

It was an October night, and the Allen brothers were returning from having a drink at the Red Lion at Beckford. "Shall us?" Martin said as they passed George Bass's rickyard. "Shall us break up the thresher?"

"Oi. May as well go hungry and linger on Parish Relief," Jim answered.

The brothers fetched two pickaxes out of George Bass's barn, and they swung the axes at the newly-painted woodwork of the threshing machine. As the wood splintered into hundreds of pieces under the October moon, in a few minutes the machine lay a heap of broken wood and iron.

While the first light of morning sneaked like a thief across the rickyard, men were putting bread and cheese in their frail baskets, ready for another day's work with the threshing machine. Spider Watchet drove his little herd of cows from the brookside meadow to their stalls at Bass's farm. Spider lived in the bothy by the stables. Just a fireplace, a bunk bed, table and candlestick were his worldly goods, apart from the blankets and his working smock and Sunday smock.

"Lor's a mercy," he called at George Bass's window. "The threshing machine is smashed and 'tis all in a heap. Who could do such a thing, gaffer?"

As the "Day Men" arrived, the Allen brothers were missing. Spider's cows stood full-uddered, unmilked in the shed as he and the other men went to the Allens' cottage up Rabbit Lane. "Appears to me thay 'a done a moonlight flit. No sign of life under the thatch, gaffer," Spider said as he stood in the lane in his milking smock and wide-awake hat. "Shall I go up Bredon Hill by the firs where I know they set rabbit snares and look around?"

"No," George Bass told him, "get back and milk the cows and give them their hay. I'll fetch Archdeacon Timbrell, Chairman of the Bench."

"Who are the Parish constables this year, Bass?" Reverend Timbrell enquired.

"The Allen brothers, sir, and they are the fellows we are after."

Sam Tombs rode his horse to Tewkesbury, the road around the Hill, and found no sign of the Allen brothers. Henry Wakeman, the Beckford squire, ordered his coachman to drive through Ashton and Elmley to Pershore bridge and look out for the Allens who might be going on a barge from there to the Severn and Bristol.

No one knew what became of Martin and Jim Allen. It was one of those mysteries unsolved, unanswered. Their parents were dead, and cousins in the villages could give no lead which way they travelled that October night. It's possible they crossed the wooded Cotswolds to Lechlade and boarded a boat which took butter down the Thames to London.

Change had not yet reached Ashton. Squire Baldwyn had a threshing floor in the big black and white half timbered barn at the Manor. A straw-thatched barn with double doors on either side, wide enough and tall enough to take a loaded farm waggon. Here Fred Dunn and Alf Stubbs, two of his workers, swung the threshing flail from Michaelmas until the cuckoo came.

The hand-turned winnowing machine stood in battleship grey paint near the sacks of threshed corn. A bushel measure and a dead weight weighing machine were alongside while the threshed straw and wheat chaff were in two bays of the barn. The straw stacked high in tied boltings or bundles, while the cream-coloured chaff blew about the place every time one of the massive doors were opened. Fred and Alf, after the corn had been cleaned of chaff by the winnowing machine, filled the sacks with four bushel measures full of grain until each sack tipped the scales at two hundredweights and one quarter.

"'Tis to be hoped that the Squire won't buy one of them machines like the one they smashed at Beckford, you," Fred said to Alf as he cut the straw bond of another sheaf and put the open sheaf on the floor.

Alf grinned at his neighbour and work mate and said, "The Allen brothers made firewood out a that 'un, didn't um?"

CHAPTER
FIVE

Jim Dance, the
Squire's Groom

Jim Dance came to work for the Squire after being a strapper, or under groom, for a gentleman near Birmingham.

The Squire had recently built some new hunting stables. Very up to date for the early half of the nineteenth century they were. The Victorian brick building with a tallet, or loft, above for the hay and clover, was tiled with cream-glazed tiles, while the separate stalls for the hunters were partitioned with sturdy iron railings above the boarded sections. This gave the hunting horses a draught-proof stall, and kept them apart, though in contact with their stable mates through the bars.

The groom's living quarters were next door to this building. A spacious bed-sitting room, with a fireplace for cooking and heating, had a clean whitewashed plaster ceiling and a sash window. The walls were lined with match boarding, stained a light oak colour. I'm sure Jim Dance had two chairs, a table and a bed. The room was lit at night from an oil lamp which swung on a broken plough trace from the ceiling. At the far corner of Jim's room was a wide door leading into the harness room.

In here the polished hunting saddles and bridles hung from the walls. The gleam of brass and silver, for some of his harness was silver mounted, and the smell of harness oil were two things which gave an impression that Jim Dance cared for the harness as he cared for the Squire's hunters. In the harness room, on the one wall, there was a locked cupboard. This was the medicine cupboard where drenches and salves, medicines and embrocations were kept to treat sick horses. Not only horse medicines were kept in the cupboard, but remedies for ailing stock of all kinds: cattle, sheep and pigs.

You see, Jim had served at his last place with a man who was known as a cow doctor. Though unqualified, this man had a good insight into veterinary practice and when he gave up work, he gave Jim his books, books well worn and thumb marked. These books not only had the printed cures for cattle, but on the bare pages at the back Jim's tutor had written in his own hand prescriptions which he had proved for the treatment of livestock.

It's odd really that I found these old books belonging to Jim Dance in the tallet above the stable. Many grooms followed Jim but Jim had hidden the two books *The Cattle Doctor* and *The Farrier* under a shelf near the gaping hole where the hay and clover was pitched down into the racks, racks made of ornate cast iron above the iron mangers and water troughs. So the dusty volumes of early nineteenth-century veterinary remedies are preserved. With the books was an old copy book with Jim's remedies written in copper-plate writing and a diary of the successes he had in treating cattle of all kinds.

Jim Dance spent so many hours, in fact many nights in April and May when the Squire's mares were foaling, sitting by a log fire just waiting until he heard the whinny of a mare about to give birth to a foal, and it was here he wrote his diary and filled in his own remedies for ailing livestock.

It was in November when Squire Baldwyn bought two hundred ewes from Stratford-on-Avon. They were a pretty sight when the drover and his dog drove them up the Groaten Lane to their pasture in the Leasow field on Bredon Hill. Fred Dunn looked after them for a few weeks, but there was little shepherding to be done in November for the ewes were already in lamb and the blue arsed fly, as Fred called it, had given up striking the sheep with fly blows when the frosts and fogs of approaching winter veiled the fields. Just a journey in the morning to count the sheep and see that none were cast on their backs, then a small ration of oats and beans in troughs.

Meanwhile Squire Baldwyn advertised for an experienced shepherd, and that was how Walter Peart from Somerset came to the village to look after the sheep on the Hill. He was used to hitching arable sheep in hurdle pens on turnips and swedes in his own county. His way of talking confounded the natives of the village. They just could not understand the Somerset accent which was quite broad.

"The 'Hims' and 'Hers' he uses instead of 'His' and 'She's' sort a baffles me, you," Fred Dunn said to Alf Stubbs.

"Oi, 'tis amus like the folk from the Forest a Dean," Alf replied. "'S marnin' Walter spoke about 'Thick Mow' and I looked at un and said, 'Don't myun the hay rick, you?' and dall my rags if I wasn't right."

The new shepherd looked at the ewes with a critical eye, enquiring of Mr. Baldwyn where they came from.

"Stratford," the Squire said. "Off good grass keep."

Walter caught one with his crook in the hurdled pen on the Leasow and ran his hand under the ewe's jaw. He found a lump under the jaw. He looked at her eyes and pulled the lids back. Quietly he said to the Squire, "Off wet land, I recon, gaffer, and it's been a wet summer."

The Squire eyed the flock and said, "A pretty good bunch of Cotswold ewes, ay, shepherd."

"Yes, they are, master, but I'm afraid of the rot after the wet summer. The liver rot."

The Squire always celebrated Christmas on January 6th, or Old Christmas Day. "We have our Christmas on January 6th and that's the right day you know," he told Walter Peart, "because the thorn doesn't bloom until then. No doubt you have seen the Glastonbury thorn in Somerset, shepherd?" The shepherd nodded. The Squire described a visit he made there when he was a young man and saw the thorn in bloom on Old

Christmas Day. "These ewes now, shepherd. Are they in good order for lambing?" the Squire asked him.

"I must tell you, sir. I've buried one and I opened her before, and her liver was full of rot."

"Worrying," the master of the Manor said. "I'll have a word with Jim Dance. He's knowledgeable about disease."

Liver fluke or rot is a difficult disease to diagnose early enough, as its progress is very slow. The animal often stays away from the flock, shaking its head with its ears depressed. It's easy to walk up and catch it, as its eyes are dull and watery and the eyelids are swollen and the lips and gums are pale. The wool loses its brightness and comes away from the skin easily, and often there's the tell-tale lump the shepherd had looked for under the ewe's jaw.

Outside the hunting stable the Squire's groom was walking towards the door carrying a brush and curry comb. Jim was a spare little man, smart in his breeches and gaiters and fancy waistcoat, well groomed himself, and hatless, his black hair just greying at the sides.

"Have you anything the shepherd can give the ewes on the Hill, Dance? About a dozen of them have liver fluke, or rot as the shepherd calls it. Look it up while I'm away, because I have to be in Evesham this morning," the Squire said.

"You are going to Evesham, master? Could you get me something in town?" Jim Dance asked the Squire.

"Yes, Dance. What is it?"

"Soft soap," Jim replied. "I'm right out."

Now Squire Baldwyn had a great sense of humour and was a man who knew pretty well what was going on on the estate. He was aware more than his men realised of the folk who were out to sponge on his generosity and, at times, literally to rob him. This is a common occurrence in situations where the employer spends a great deal of time with horse and hounds, and with rod and gun. The Squire managed the farm without a bailiff. Several had been employed by him, but he now relied on his shepherd, his waggoner and his cowman to keep an eye on the regular running of his farms.

"Soft soap, ay, Dance. Soft soap, ay," he said over and over again. "Now there's quite a lot of soft soap used on my farms."

Jim Dance knew what he meant and replied, "I suppose there is, sir."

While Squire Baldwyn was in Evesham, Jim Dance looked through his veterinary books in the section marked "sheep". He found several recipes so from his medicine cupboard he prepared the one he favoured as follows:

> 2 ounces of powdered charcoal
> 1 ounce of ginger
> 1 ounce of golden seal
> 1 pound of oatmeal

This was to be fed to the sheep a handful a day. If the ewes had lost their cud, or rumination had ceased, the mixture without the oatmeal was to be given in half a pint of horsemint tea, the dose being one teaspoonful.

(Horsemint grew readily in the Squire's ditch above the duck pond.)

A thirsty animal with high-coloured urine was to have a pint of cleavers boiled in water. Cleavers again were plentiful in the cornfield, called by most farm men "hayriff".

Jim Dance took a supply of the first mixture up to the shepherd on the Hill. The shepherd had folded a dozen or so of the ewes in the barn and was feeding sainfoin hay, bright and sweet, and a few sliced turnips with some cotton and linseed cake. The rest of the flock were moved to pastures between the stone walls near the Parish Quarry. Here the land was near the one-thousand-foot contour and Shepherd Peart knew from past experience that the higher and drier his sheep lay, the less was the risk of liver rot.

Jim and the shepherd fed the ewes in the barn with the mixture and drenched a couple of the worst afflicted ones with the cleavers drink. Jim studied his books by the fire in the evening and was ready to mix yet another medicine for his master's ewes if the first lot failed.

This was Calley's Red Salve:

> 4 ounces of best honey
> 2 ounces of burnt alum
> ½ a pound of American bole
> and enough fish oil to make a salve

Whether it was Jim Dance's medicine or not, Uncle Jim told me that the Squire's sheep mostly recovered.

It's so hard to tell because these ewes were fed with nutritious food and that alone in a warm barn was a help towards their recovery.

What a character Jim Dance was and what an asset to the Squire in the days when vets were still mainly horse doctors and rarely treated cows and sheep. A man of Jim's ability was vital in the everyday management of farm stock.

Uncle Jim's account of the groom's work at the manor farms comes chiefly from Grandfather William Archer. You see, William Archer and Jim Dance lived close to one another after Jim's marriage to Tilda. Jim met Tilda at the Manor when she was a dairy maid for Squire Henry Baldwyn. When Tilda married him, Jim moved from the groom's room and they lived in a little brick and tiled cottage near the Manor Cider Mill. Tilda was a keen Nonconformist, singing solos at the cottage meetings in the village attended by Jim Dance and William Archer. Jim wasn't very religious, Uncle said, but he tolerated her hymn-singing and her harmonium playing in the cottage and at the meetings.

It's strange how the record handed down from father to son still exists of the quality of Tilda's voice. Some said she was the highest soprano that ever sung at a cottage meeting in this corner of the country. It's said she could make the dainty glasses on dining tables vibrate to her top notes. Uncle told me that he often sat in front of Tilda at meetings when she was in her eighties, after the Chapel was built. He described her voice to me as that of a nightingale.

Some years after Shepherd Peart's problem with the liver fluke among the ewes on the Hill, Jim Dance was faced with another problem. Foot and mouth disease. Stockman and farmer used to live in dread when the pasture fields shone in the autumn sunshine. They shone in an ominous sort of way. They shone with tiny cobwebs covering the grass like gossamer, the little droplets of moisture clinging to the cobwebs. It's often been said that this is just the thing that causes husk or hoose. The symptoms are shortness of breath, an attempt to cough, and general catarrh. In fact the real cause is a small worm in the windpipe which irritates the breathing passages.

Jim used his favourite remedy for husk. A well-thumbed page in his book of cures is marked by him, while his diary records the recipe which had the best results. The ingredients, as listed in Jim's remedy book, were:

> 2 ounces of elecampane
> 1 ounce of salt of wormwood
> 1 ounce of liquorice powder
> 1 ounce of sweet spirits of nitre
> ½ ounce of aethrop's mineral

The last four he would get from the apothecary, but elecampane, with its long broad leaves, whitish-green with a grey underside, "groweth in most grounds and shadowy places almost in every county of this land", according to a herbal of 1809, which goes on to say: "The decoction of the roots in wine, or the juice taken therein, killeth and driveth forth all manner of worms in the belly, stomach and maw . . . the root boiled well in vinegar, beaten afterwards, and made into an ointment with hog's suet, or oil of trotters, is an excellent remedy for scab or itch in young or old."

A useful plant, elecampane. I don't know if Jim Dance ever tried his concoctions on himself, but this is what his remedy book records under that list of five ingredients which were his tried and tested cure for the husk:

This is a powerful and very efficacious medicine for the lungs, it destroys the ill habit thereof, and evacuates the offending humours from the pulmonic vessels. It eases, warms and comforts, and is a good diuretic. It will rouse the spirits when depressed by insensible perspiration.

It's hard to know how much good this concoction did because Jim also poured vinegar into a hot brick held by tongs under the beast's nose as an inhalant. He used another remedy on stubborn cases, a remedy which stood the test of time over many years. Up each nostril was poured a tablespoonful of the mixture to kill the worm in the windpipe. The mixture consisted of linseed oil, turpentine and hartshorn. This does work, I have proved it.

When foot and mouth disease struck the Baldwyn herd, the affected animals were isolated from the rest so that it didn't spread. Squire Baldwyn farmed four farms in the village so that when one farm was affected

41

he was able to isolate the outbreak from the rest. There was no cure for the affected animals, who quickly lost condition and would have died but for the constant attention of the Squire's men.

Jim Dance helped Fred Dunn to feed the animals on a liquid food. They made sloppy bran mashes and barley mashes. They also made a kind of tea from sweet hay which they poured down the animals' throats. It was difficult to get them to swallow when their mouths and tongues were ulcerated, so this called for another of Jim's ideas. They put an old boot into each cow's mouth, a boot with the toe cut away. Then they slowly poured the liquid feed into the upper part of the boot. The use of linseed tea helped to keep the cattle alive, as did the deep bed of warm straw to bed down on.

Was it worth it to keep sick animals alive? Perhaps, if we consider the financial side of it, no, but the Squire and Jim and Fred looked at the problem in a different light. They were intent on saving the life of the cattle, regardless of the time and money involved, because they considered that for animals to die from disease on the farm was not right if the lives could be saved. It's true, that when the cattle began to recover, as many of them did, they were skin and bones, without milk, without meat, but a summer grazing the brookside meadows would soon put a shine on their coats and flesh on their backs.

So Jim Dance was remembered not only as a groom, the Squire's groom, but as a vet without letters, a cow doctor who asked his master to bring him some soft soap from Evesham.

CHAPTER
SIX

Hobbledehoys with a Scythe

Grandfather William Archer was broken in to mowing with the scythe when he was a youth of sixteen, in the early 1840s. The old men called a scythe a "dismal" and what an apt description. Surely there are few implements of agriculture that can give the worker the kind of backache which he gets while using the scythe. But the eight-shilling-a-week labourers on the land, who had spent a winter and spring on the soil of Ashton where the clay clings to the hob-nailed boots like putty, were eager to get away to the hay fields where the mowing grass was ready for the blade of the scythe in June.

So William, Dan, Neal and Long Fred prepared to go mowing on the Tewkesbury Hams. The men who left Ashton were normally men from the Manor, but were allowed to be away for the month of June in Tewkesbury. The truth was that the mowing at Tewkesbury was piece work at so much per acre, and the thought of some extra money did appeal to William and his friends.

These river meadows, or hams, are the biggest tracks of pasture land in the district. The Bredon Ham which runs from the Manor to the River Avon is flat and vast. It floods in winter so that the silt from the swollen river gives a kind of fertilising dressing made up of the riches of the land carried down from the Evesham Vale. Early heavy crops of grass grow here when the May sun warms the land, still moist from the winter flood.

Now Great Grandfather was a good hand at mowing with a scythe. He mowed the Squire's fields with the older men, but they didn't start until June 26th. From that date he worked six days a week for the Squire and young William would be back from Tewkesbury by then.

The evening before the eight-mile walk to the Tewkesbury Hams was spent in Long Fred's hovel at the bottom of his garden. Long Fred was married, as was Neal. He was a man of about forty and an expert at mowing.

It suited him to take what he called a couple of colts or hobbledehoys, like William and Dan, and put them through their paces in the hay field. In Fred's hovel the two men and two hobbledehoys prepared for the mowing. The scythes were sharpened on the grindstone and the blades were pitched or angled at the right pitch. Great hip briars had been cut from a field hedge to use as sheaths for the scythe blades. These hip briars were cut the same length as the blade, then they were carefully split in two. Half a briar was secured on to the cutting edge of the scythe blade, forming a shield to protect the blade from damage while they travelled to their work and also to protect the users from being cut by the sharp knife edge, or their dogs as they travelled with them.

The early Monday morning walk to Tewkesbury took the four men through Teddington and Ashchurch, then along Barton Street where the great Abbey tower could be seen, square, Norman and grey in the morning light. At the bottom of the High Street where the Bredon road leaves the Worcester road, Carrants Brook flows under a bridge on the last lap of its winding journey from Ashton to the River Avon.

William, Dan, Neal and Long Fred found Farmer Attwood waiting by a gate at the entrance of the big Ham Meadow. He showed the men into a stable with a couple of horse standings well littered with straw.

"That's your bed for tonight, men, and don't light your tobacco pipes in there among the straw."

Next door to the stable was an empty harness room and a couple of benches where the men could eat their food and drink their cider. It was in here where Farmer Attwood brought them their breakfast next morning and filled their wooden cider bottles. Before work began, he put a loaf of bread on one of the benches and a lump of fat bacon. From a golden-coloured stone jar he filled their gallon bottles with cider.

"Now," he said, addressing Long Fred, "you have a couple of hobbledehoys with you this year, so I want the grass cut short. No long stubbles mind."

Fred nodded as he said, "I'll watch 'um, gaffer."

When the scythes were whetted until the blades were sharp enough to shave with, Long Fred struck off clock-wise around the meadow followed by William and Dan; Neal bringing up the rear. "Now, young fellas," Long Fred said to Dan and William, "keep the knoll down."

The knoll is the heel or part of the scythe next to the sned or handle. By keeping it down low, the point of the scythe does not stick into the earth when the blade swishes through the dewy grass, exposing the bare ground beneath a short yellow stubble. What a thrill William and Dan had that day in June to see the swath fall behind the blade and see the slugs and other insects exposed to the sunshine after their long shelter in the ley in dewy darkness. Neal's blade shaved the grass closer and closer to Dan's heels. He had to stop mowing until the young haymaker had taken some more sweeps with his scythe.

"The scythes need touching up with the whetstone," William Archer said as he felt the edge of his blade with his thumb.

Long Fred looked at William's scythe with the eye of an expert. "Allus put a long edge on the blade with the whetstone, William bwoy," he said.

Taking the scythe from young William, Long Fred stood it up with the end of the sned on the ground and cleared the grass from the blade. He then took a whetstone from the leather holster on the back of his broad belt to sharpen William's scythe. The stone on the steel blade made a pleasant sound as Long Fred stroked the curved knife of the scythe until the cutting edge shone like silver, a quarter of an inch of sharpened steel.

It's a long way round the Tewkesbury Ham, but by twilight the four Ashton men had made a pattern of cut grass, while the sunshine had partly made the swathes cut in the morning into hay. Walking back to the stable, William smelt the wonderful scent of the partly-made swath when the clover and vetches are wilted and the rye grass is dried and the green herbage has turned to a bluish grey.

"Good gaffer, Master Attwood is," Long Fred said as they entered the harness room. "Some farmers give only bread and cheese, and the cheese is that hard it needs cutting with the coulter of a plough." Carpenter's mutton, they used to call the twopence a pound farmhouse cheese. "Oi, Neal, you know what your old dad used to say in the hay field?"

Neal was out with the rhyme before Long Fred could recite it. "Ham and eggs mind your legs, Bread and cheese take your ease."

This little ditty showed how way back in Neal's father's time men worked well when the living was good, but on bread and cheese the pace was slower. So the mowing progressed by the acre with Farmer Attwood supplying good cider, good bread, good bacon and milk puddings to the four Ashton men.

CHAPTER
SEVEN

Shin-kicking
Champion

How true it is that nothing equips a man better for rural sports than swinging a scythe from daylight to dark in the hayfield. It's said that the dismal flexes every sinew in the human body.

William Archer and young Dan had been taken to Dovers Hill near Chipping Campden by their fathers to watch the Cotswold Olympics there when they were small boys. This experience sparked off something in their young minds, so that when they grew into hobbledehoys they too were eager to pit their strength against the youth of the Cotswolds and the Evesham Vale.

The sports on Dovers Hill had a long pedigree. In the early nineteenth century the games were advertised in a local paper as follows:

That noble, generous, heroic Mr. Robert Dover instituted the mighty celebrated and renowned Olympic Games in 1612 for which this festival claims precedence of all others, now patronised by Church and State and esteemed by all brave and true and free spirited Britons who admire the many exercises for what this kingdom is so justly famed.

Two dozen belts to be wrestled for.
To contend for these the Dons of high blood and mettle are required to be on the turf.
Dancing for ribbons.
Jumping in sacks.
A grand display of Back Swords.

Rules for Horse Races
Proper persons to keep the course clear.
All stray dogs seen on the course will be destroyed.
A charge of one guinea will be made to sell beer or wines from a booth or shed, paid to the conductor of the sports.
There will be an excellent company of comedians at the Old Theatre, Campden, each evening.
Balls and Concerts each day and Ordinaries each day.

"Ordinaries" would be a public mid-day dinner, as was common in market towns on market day. I like the wording at the end:

"The silent evening to be ushered in by a merry dance at nine o'clock. God Save the Queen."

It's debatable whether Back Sword play was even more damaging to the players than Shin Kicking. The rules of Back Sword Fencing were as follows:

First of all an arena was marked out forming a circle. This was done by drawing a line of whitewash on the turf. The challengers threw their coats into the ring, a gesture which meant that they were willing to take on all-comers. The referee stood by as the men struck at each other with the pointed, peeled withy sticks. When one man drew blood by striking his opponent on the head, the referee stopped the bout and examined the head of the one who had been struck to make sure blood was coming from a wound inflicted by his opponent who stuck his pointed stick in the ground. The winner received five shillings and the champion of the day was given a belt.

It was on Dovers Hill that William Archer and Dan first indulged in the rough sport of Shin Kicking. They were soon beaten by the old hands, notably, George Perry, known as the "Bully of Stoulton Wake". The rules were varied, but it was generally considered that to put one's opponent on the grass twice in three rounds secured a victory. Also called Booty Play, Shin Kicking was wrestling for one's boots, and what boots! One writer describes the boots as shod with heavy nails and with metal toe caps or tips somewhat outspread, or pointing out a little past the toe of the boot. If the tips, which often came to a point, were made of brass, the injuries dealt out to the opposing player could be serious. As the men held each others shoulders they tried to ward off kicks on their shins and drop a kick on their opponent's.

On Bredon Hill summit across the Vale from the Cotswolds, the Whitsuntide games were held each year.

Perhaps this rural arena had not been the scene of competition for as long as Dovers Hill, but who knows. Here, as there, men showed their skill at back swords and shin kicking. The girls danced for ribbons, the men fought for belts.

Picture the scene on Bredon summit on Trinity Monday, the Monday after Whitsun, in fact, the Monday after Dovers Hill Olympics on the Friday. Bredon Hill stands, as is often said, like a stranded whale between the Cotswold Hills and the Malverns, an outcrop of the Vale of Evesham capped with little spinneys of beech and plantations of larch and fir. At the summit, where Squire Parsons built his folly around 1800, there is a natural amphitheatre, relic of an iron age fortress. The turf is springy, the grass is short and competes with wild thyme to provide a bare living for the sheep. The farmers used to bring their cobs and hunters here at Whitsun to race them over the gorse-thatched hurdle fences for prizes.

The boundaries of this arena are great barrow-mounds of earth, like giant potato burys. These formed a natural frame for the sports and a shelter to the spectators. In one coppice close by, the fiddlers played their instruments and the girls danced for the ribbons. Fiddlers' Nap it's still called, after the old fiddlers of the hill villages. There are fourteen of these, all linked by a winding road under the Hill, but more important, all the villagers had access to the Hill itself by footpath or cart track.

In the arena by the Folly, William Archer took on a seasoned shin kicker from Kemerton village and lost.

Standing by was Joseph Payne, a local blacksmith and Parish constable.

"Thee come along a me, William boy," he said after William had been floored twice by the Kemerton man. "Come down to the smithy, boy, and I'll teach tha a few wrinkles."

William was amazed at what he saw that Monday in the village. On the anvil near the forge, Joe Payne lay bare a leg and beat his shin with a blacksmith's hammer. Then he beat the other leg. It didn't seem to hurt the blacksmith. Then, turning to young William, he said, "I hadn't better hammer thy legs today 'cos they 'ull be main sore after the pasting you had from the Kemerton chap."

William took off his leather gaiters which he wore over his corduroy breeches and showed Joe the scars he had received in the three rounds of wrestling with his opponent. Joe felt the shins of young William and said, "They be as soft as a bit of silk. Come into my house, boy, and we'll dress them with my special cure."

In Joe's kitchen William's shins were anointed with pure malt vinegar from a little barrel he kept beside the barrels of cider and home-brewed beer. Joe then took a quart bottle and filled it with vinegar for William to take home to dress his shins with every week. "William," Joe said, "I got a lot a faith in thee as a shin kicker so keep your legs suppled with vinegar and come along to the blacksmith's shop as often as you can and I'll hammer thee legs gently at first."

William was taken by the old man's words and promised to do just that. "George Perry won the belt on Bredon Hill today and next year it's your turn," Joe said. "Now, don't let me down, 'cos I'll put some money on you and we'll share, see."

At home when William's shins were getting tougher he practised the rough wrestling with young Dan. Dan was a game sort of lad who excelled in the ring at bare-fisted boxing. He won so many fights in Townsend Field on Boxing Day against young men from the Hill villages who came to the annual Sparrow Shoot.

What a strange custom this bare-fisted fighting was. The men came to Ashton on Boxing Day as they met on Bredon Hill on Trinity Monday, from Elmley, Kersoe, Little and Great Comberton, Eckington, Bredon, Hardwick, Bredons Norton, Westmancote, Kemerton, Overbury, Conderton, Beckford and Grafton.

Although the villages were all part of a circle at the foot of the hill, the villagers thought of the folk from the next Parish as foreigners only to be met with at the Hill Sports, at Boxing Day and at Evesham Mop. If they didn't fight tooth and nail on these days, it was said the beer and cider was not strong enough.

A year after young William's defeat on Bredon Hill he was matched again against George Perry, the Bully of Stoulton Wake. Alf Stubbs and Fred Dunn, the Squire's men, and Spider Watchet, who worked for Squire Wakeman, walked up Bredon Hill across Holcombe Nap and Great Hill, past the parish quarry to the Folly with William that Monday morning. Squire Baldwyn had given his men the day off after milking, for he himself was racing his hunter against horses from other villages, and it was his groom, Jim Dance, who was to be referee for both the shin kicking and the prize fights. Young Dan had already won his bout when he took on an Elmley chap prize fighting for a belt.

Joe Payne, the blacksmith, who had now given up the somewhat dangerous sport of shin kicking, was sitting on the edge of the arena. He would take off his gaiters and show the young men the injuries he had suffered, injuries from the metal tips of the shin kickers' boots. Proud he was of the belts he had won, but now his prospective champion was William Archer, and he had tutored him well.

George Perry walked up from the other side of the Hill, having come over the fields crossing the Avon at Eckington Bridge. A tall angular man was George, long in the legs and shod with wicked-looking metal-tipped boots. William was short, square shouldered, a stocky man who said he could lift a sack of wheat in his teeth — teeth he kept to his death at seventy-three.

"I'll doust ya, young William," George Perry called from his seat near the Folly tower. "Doust ya" or "Dust you" was an expression used by the Olympic contestants of Dovers Hill and Bredon.

William drank a couple of pints of cider from barrels provided by Squire Parsons, Squire Martin and Squire Baldwyn. Completely relaxed, he threw his jacket into the ring as a challenge to George Perry. George ambled across and took up his position as he had done for so many encounters at Whitsun and after.

I suppose all the men from the Hill villages who could climb Bredon that day were there to witness what Joe Payne reckoned would be a victory for the Ashton fellow, William Archer. "Let Perry do the kicking," Joe advised William. "Keep him warded off for a couple of rounds," he said. "Then on the third go in and hammer him when his wind is gone."

William took heed and kept his now tough shins away from the vicious spikes of George's shoes. At the third round, when neither man had fallen, William held tight to George and, kicking with both feet, had him down. Then a second time George Perry was down on Bredon's springy turf, and Jim Dance proclaimed William Archer the winner. After beating George Perry, no one was prepared to wrestle with him and he was presented with a decorated leather belt by a gentleman from Woolass Hall.

After drinking cider until it almost oozed from their ears, the Ashton men threw at the coconuts. William paid the man at the booth one shilling and waited for tenpence change.

The man in charge said, "You gave me sixpence, young fella."

Sam Tombs the Bailiff from Beckford spoke up. "Give the lad tenpence change."

The coconut man refused and half a dozen cider peart Ashton men rolled his coconuts down the steep slope of the hill near the Banbury Stone. The tired and cider-fuddled men spent the night on straw in Great Hill Barn, but were all at work at the Manor Farm next morning, where Jim Dance told them that the horse he had trained was ridden to victory by the Squire, winning by a distance from a Woolass Hall horse.

It was too late for William to challenge the Cotswold men at Dovers Hill that year, but the following year, much to his mother's annoyance, William had a week at the sports on Vale and Hill. He went to Evesham on Whit Monday, Childswickham Wake on Tuesday, Broadway Wake on Wednesday, on Thursday and Friday to Dovers Hill Games and Snowshill Wake on Saturday. Not always winning at Booty Play, but he did collect a number of belts and a few sovereigns, remaining for years the Champion of Bredon Hill.

Like Joe Payne, William carried the scars of these bouts to his grave. He too took his leggins or gaiters off after a day's work on his holding or in the Squire's fields, and showed the marks of Booty Play to the family. It was not just the scars inflicted by the metal-tipped boots of his opponents, William's shins were marked for life where eight gaiter buttons on each leg had been indented into his flesh. Yes, sixteen button marks could be seen as permanent blue scars up his legs. The day he died, these marks were showing quite plainly when he was laid in the elm coffin ready for St. Barbara's churchyard.

CHAPTER
EIGHT

William Archer's Stocking

When Benedict Wakeman died at Beckford Hall, the Ashton-under-Bredon part of the estate was sold by Walter and Philadelphia Wakeman. Walter had married Philadelphia Pasmore and it is recorded that three children were born by the body of Walter on the body of Philadelphia. Unfortunately the children died in infancy, and that influenced Walter to sell a part of his estate in Ashton in 1848.

The Baldwyn estate increased as a result. William Crump farmed Dyers Farm, one hundred and thirty-five acres at £220 per annum rent. The land included Furze Hill, the Groaten, the Rails, Calf Rails (Great Carrants, Little Carrants), adjoining Grandfather's holding, Stone Bridge Piece and the Dewrests adjoining Dewrest Lane. News Farm was rented by Thomas Martin, ninety-seven acres at £175 per annum, which included Townsend Close, the Dean, and Thornhursts Sallow Beds.

Stephen Baldwyn, a relative of the Squire, farmed Ashton Manor Farm and Kersoe Farm, Crooked

Holbrook, Catbrain, Tear Coat and Van Diemen's Land. Van Dieman's Land and Crooked Holbrook were reckoned to be the property of John Baldwyn, a younger son of Squire Henry Baldwyn.

To stake his claim for these two fields at Kersoe John got James Bayliss to make a statutory declaration to the effect that they belonged to him. It appeared that the selling of Wakeman's land at Ashton was a complex affair. David Drinkwater's sisters, Suzan and Elizabeth, bought pasture land, then sold again to Bernard Baldwyn, another of the Squire's relations. William Spires, shoemaker, late of Ashton, but living at Hemel Hempstead, sold the Hams to David Drinkwater. The change-over of 1848 meant that some of Squire Wakeman's employees moved from Beckford to Ashton and in the ten years from 1841 to 1851 the population rose from three hundred and forty-two to three hundred and ninety-six.

Some of the heavy clay land on News Farm was waterlogged and needed draining. The Squire engaged William Archer to drain the land at the north end of the village on contract, and asked him to get another man to work with him. It so happened that Spider Watchet, who had been Squire Wakeman's cowman, was now looking for a job elsewhere. The Wakemans did keep the Hall but gave up their milking herd. Spider was a bachelor who lodged at Beckford but teamed up with William to drain the clay land at Ashton, where he was parish clerk. He had been grave digger at Beckford, but owed his promotion to a good word put in for him with

Archdeacon Timbrell by Sam Tombs, the Squire of Beckford's bailiff.

"Watchet," the Vicar had said, "I want a parish clerk for Ashton church. Tombs, he recommended you."

"Well, sir, I can read and write and am in the church band, as you know. I play the big bass viol," Spider replied with a certain shyness.

"That's why I've asked you, isn't it, man. You knowing Tate and Brady's Psalms in verse. You're appointed. Understand?"

"Yes, sir," Spider answered. "I'll do my best, sir."

So Spider had become the young clerk of St. Barbara's after the death of old Ben Stephens, who had held office until he died at ninety-four. Old Ben had continued to come to church on two sticks, when he was unable to feed himself, being fed by his old sister with a spoon. A remarkable man.

"Now, Watchet, you know what I expect from you. You will make the beeswax candles for the altar at home in the moulds Stephens used. The tallow candles in the aisle, you will keep the wicks clipped."

"Yes, sir," Spider replied, "and am I to say amen during service as Ben Stephens did?"

"Of course. You will get written instructions from me and attend to notices. See that the church is kept clean and tidy. Be present at funerals."

"Yes, sir," Spider said.

Thomas and Elizabeth Archer died in 1847, leaving a cottage belonging to William Henry Baldwyn near Townsend Close empty. William Archer was twenty-one and he had saved some money in a stocking, put by for the time when he would get married. For a couple of years he had been courting Mary Ann Harris from Alderton. His smallholding at Carrants Field lay in a direct line from the village to Alderton. When he finished work there on Saturday nights he walked across Dewrest Lane, following the Old Saltway to Didcot, then skirted Alderton Hill to the village.

It was here that Mary Ann lived with her widowed mother. She was in service at the Manor but began work in the kitchen of one of the big houses at Pitville in Cheltenham. Mary Ann had received some schooling and was able to read and write and knew her Bible. William would persuade her to read the newspaper to him. He was interested in news of local court cases, the reports of poaching and the price of corn and cattle.

Mary Ann was a member of the Church of England and although William attended the Methodist meetings, he had been baptised by Archdeacon Timbrell. "I suppose the Reverend Timbrell will have to be told of my intentions to marry you, Mary," William said when the harvest was over in 1848.

"Go and see him, Will. I'm sure he will be civil to you," Mary said.

So William called and visited the venerable man at Beckford Vicarage. The Archdeacon had moved there some little time before from Bretforton when the Church Law insisted that a vicar must live in the parish where he was responsible for the souls of the people. In any case, the residence at Bretforton belonging to the benefice was in a most dilapidated state. It could not be made suitable for an incumbent and the property was sold for £200 and converted into two cottages. So Reverend Timbrell came to Beckford where he added one wing after another to the small vicarage until it began to look like a hospital with wards. Not that Thomas Archer had complained, as it had made plenty of business for a master carpenter.

His youngest brother, William, was treated with respect by the old Archdeacon, who promised to have the banns called for the wedding and arranged for one of his curates to perform the ceremony on the Saturday afternoon planned. "You are one of the company who gather in Mr. Heek's house at the Methodist meeting, aren't you, Archer?" the parish priest asked.

"Yes, sir, I am one of that society," William answered.

"I have no time for the followers of Wesley, you know, and when you are married I shall expect you and your wife, who is an Anglican, to come to St. Barbara's church."

William was a little baffled by the directness of the parson's words. He nodded, cap in hand, in the hall of the vicarage and then words came to him, words which were so true to William Archer. "You see, sir, I'm an uneducated man, no scholar and the Methodist meeting seems right for the likes of me."

"Ah, the doggerel in the hymns, I suppose, and the Love Feasts instead of Communion," the vicar replied with a laugh.

William agreed that the hymn-singing around the harmonium in company with fifteen to twenty other villagers put heart into him on Sunday nights before his work began at six o'clock on Monday morning.

"You will be married according to the Prayer Book," was the Archdeacon's parting shot that Saturday evening at the vicarage.

The following Sunday the banns were read at St. Barbara's church, Ashton-under-Hill, and at Alderton parish church, and on the Monday night William went to the house of Long Fred's father, John Panting, the village tailor, to be measured for a new suit.

This suit lasted William as Sunday best for most of his married life. It was grey, a dark grey, what could be described as Methodist grey, made of Cotswold tweed with four buttons on the jacket and a vertical button hole in the middle of his buttoned waistcoat, to slip the tee piece of his silver watch chain through. The trousers were lined with cotton, full fronted with buttons up each side. The back of the waistcoat was of a silky material which shone like satin. Never before had William worn a suit so genteel.

When John had finished it, William took it over to Alderton, packed in brown paper in his frail basket, and showed it to Mary Ann. "Now, Will, try it on and see what a smart chap our Mary is to marry," her mother said.

In the wash-house at the Alderton cottage of Mrs. Harris, William put on his new suit while Mary Ann slipped on her bridal gown. "There's a fine couple," Mrs. Harris said with tears in her eyes. "And to think that my man, God bless him, married me in his cords as he came from the hay field. How did you manage to buy such a suit, Will?" she said.

"'Tis the stocking, Mother, and there's still some silver and a little gold in there," William replied. He explained how some years ago his mother had knitted him a long narrow stocking, no bigger round than a sausage, just big enough to hold half crowns. He then told his future mother-in-law how he had picked a good crop of strawberries on Carrants Field that summer and how Mr. Rogers, who ran the carrier's cart to the Rose and Crown at Evesham, took his fruit to the Smithfield in the High Street. Mr. Rogers brought back the money to Ashton every week and deducted his carriage.

When the wedding day arrived William walked down Ashton village with Spider Watchet, his companion worker at Squire Baldwyn's land draining, who he had chosen to be witness or best man for his marriage to Mary Ann. William's mother and Mrs. Harris sat together in the church, clutching the prayer books they had used since their Confirmation.

As Spider Watchet and the bridegroom passed through the slip slap or kissing gate, beside the heavy iron gate with the lamp above, William said, "Look there."

"Look at what, Will?" Spider asked.

"The trees I planted. The drooping ash trees. They 'ull be a sight one day." William paused to take up a young branch of one of the drooping ash trees and shook the keys which were ripening in the autumn sun.

"Ah, a fad, I suppose, of the Squire's," Spider replied. "They 'ull never make timber, but 'ull look unkind like when they be twenty foot high."

The wedding was attended by just a knot of neighbours and friends who came to wish Mary Ann and William well. Mary Ann looked a picture in a shot silk navy dress trimmed with cream lace, and she wore cream gloves. She was attended by her one sister, Phoebe Hams.

Fred Dunn, Alf Stubbs, Jim Dance, Walter Peart and Long Fred rang the bells as William and his bride rode up the village street in Squire Baldwyn's spring cart driven by Neal Allen. At the cottage the company sat down to a meal of griskins and sparerib from a recently killed pig, runner beans and potatoes from Carrants Field, and drank the couple's health in some of William's special parsnip wine.

As the conversation got livelier and the men's faces shone like a winter sunset on a frosty night, Mary Ann begged them to go easy on the wine. She herself had signed the pledge to never touch, taste nor handle anything intoxicating; a pledge she kept until her dying day. Spider Watchet insisted on singing a song he had learnt at the White Hart, a song sung there by a traveller some years before. It went:

> I love the green fields, I love the sunshine,
> The robin with pretty red breast.
> I love pussy cat fast asleep on the mat
> But I love my dear mother the best.

At four o'clock that autumn day in Ashton a horse and tradesman's cart came up the Groaten from Evesham. The sign on the side read H. Ward, Clock maker, Gold and Silversmith, Evesham. It stopped at William Archer's cottage. Mr. Ward's man and his boy unloaded from the cart a grandfather clock, and carried it into the house where the bridal party were celebrating.

"Oh, Will, is that for us, Will? What a lovely surprise," the new bride whispered to her bridegroom.

Her mother, Mrs. Harris, threw up her hands in amazement and before William could say anything she came out with, "However did you manage to buy that, Will?"

Amid laughter Will answered just two words, "The stocking."

Out of his stocking, William told his friends, he had paid Henry Ward of Evesham five pounds for the clock. It was a real beauty as it stood near the front door in a light oak case with a porcelain face encircled with pink flowers. No one knew then how important that clock was going to be in the Archer household, for every night William opened the little door and grasped the chains pulling up the great weight, to wind up the grandfather clock when it warned for nine o'clock at four minutes to the hour. If a visitor was still in the house, William then opened the front door with these words which became well known at Archers', "I'll wish you good night for I am going to bed."

No one kept William up after nine o'clock at night.

So William and Mary Ann started their married life in a cottage big enough for a couple or even big enough for a couple and four children.

The kitchen with a stone-slabbed floor was furnished with a white scrubbed table and four chairs, while the black leaded oven grate had two hobs and above the fire various sized pot hooks were used to hang the kettle, or the frying pan, the iron pot and the iron saucepans, made with a loop opposite the handle to hook on to one of the pot hooks. The brown crock sink, used for washing clothes, pots, pans, cups and saucers, had a water bucket underneath. The water was fetched from the well. The little wash-house which formed a lean-to at the back, housed the copper boiler and a heavy mangle. Opposite this was a lead salting trough for salting flitches of bacon.

Elizabeth Archer, who had lived here for so long with Thomas until they both died in 1847, had looked after the place very well. In fact she did leave behind a couple of chairs for the little front room, a sofa and a what-not. On the what-not Mary Ann proudly placed a Worcester tea service given to them as a wedding present by Squire Baldwyn.

The staircase was steep and narrow, quite typical of farm workers' cottages of the eighteenth century. The front bedrooms were square with small windows either side of the doorway below. Grandfather's back bedroom was long and narrow like a skittle alley, giving room for two single beds. It was in the front bedroom, nearest the garden which ran alongside the road, that William had directed the big iron bedstead with brass knobs to be erected by a furnisher from Tewkesbury.

This is where William and Mary Ann began and eventually ended their married life, a life which was hard but rewarding, divided between his work on the Carrants Field holding and the hay-making, the harvesting, and draining for Squire Baldwyn.

As Christmas 1848 drew near William and Spider Watchet drained the Dean, a heavy arable field north of the village. The pay was nine pence a rope, which apparently was the same as a rod, pole or perch, five and a half yards. But the winter was wet and cold, the drains were dug three feet deep and soon filled with water. Walking home on December nights when the light became too dim to work, Spider and William often found the top soil encrusted by the evening frost. Just how bone hard clayland can become when it's frozen is amazing. "'Tis putting it up together tonight, Spider," William would say, and the freezing wind from the north soon froze their corduroy trousers which had been wet through up to their knees.

Mary Ann was worried about her husband coming home in such a state. His trousers were as stiff as a board when he entered the kitchen. "Whatever do you do to get in that state, Will?" she said.

"The money's good, Mary. Much better than the men get who are ploughing. That's partly how I filled that stocking," he replied.

"Off with your trousers," she ordered as she gave him a dry pair to put on. "I don't know," she added. "Legs scarred at shin kicking, now frozen at draining. You will suffer when you are older."

William smiled, called for his dinner from the oven, telling her he was young and strong still and still able to lift a sack of wheat in his teeth.

After tea she read her Bible to him by lamplight, then at four minutes to nine he wound up the long-cased clock. "Another day tomorrow, Mary, so let's go up the wooden hill to bed."

The candle gave a yellow light up the stairs.

CHAPTER
NINE

By Hook and By Crook

William Archer and Mary Ann were pleased when the long winter was over and the draining finished. The land at Carrants Field, apart from that which grew the strawberries and plums, had been ploughed by Alf Stubbs, the Squire's carter. William had planted his wheat and beans with a wooden setting dibber, and trenched in his potatoes with his heavy three-tined fork. He always timed his bean planting by the elm tree's progress: when the elm leaf is as big as a farthing, it's time to plant runner beans in the garden; when the elm leaf is as big as a penny, it's time to plant, if you're going to have any! was how it went.

"I don't want you to go down to the Tewkesbury Ham mowing this summer, Will," Mary Ann said in a voice which her young husband could not help take notice of.

"Why, my dear 'ooman?" he replied, knowing full well what the reason was.

"Well," she explained, "'tis like this. Now we have set up home together, I don't like the thought of you lying rough with the other fellows and me left alone in the cottage and you sleeping in a barn."

So William promised his wife that he would stay in the village for the haymaking and use his scythe in Mr. Baldwyn's meadows. The crops of hay in the Carrant Brook meadows were always heavy. The grass grew lush in the spring after the winter floods, while Squire Baldwyn's leys on the Hill had improved ever since the improver of grassland in the late eighteenth century, Mr. Stillingfleet, introduced the harvesting of grass seeds. Before then, in Great Grandfather's youth, the grass leys were planted from the grass seeds shed in the cattle mangers, with docks and thistle seeds mixed in with the clover and grasses.

The day men on the farm were paid one shilling and six pence a day while Shepherd Peart was paid eleven shillings a week. Spider Watchet stayed with William that haymaking and they were both paid two shillings and six pence an acre for mowing, with a gallon of cider each. William and Spider were able to mow an acre each a day with the scythe if they started at daybreak and mowed until the evening, earning six half crowns each a week and drinking six gallons of cider.

Harvest started when the winter-sown wheat was ready in August. The Squire's groom, true to tradition, sounded the Harvest Horn each morning at five o'clock, when any of the day men who were late to work forfeited wages at the weekend. William worked piece work, but was in the field at dawn or a little before, and worked until the edge of night, an hour after the sun had sunk down behind the Malvern Hills.

He worked with the two hooks, cutting the sheaves by hook and by crook. This made a tidier harvest than the old method when the corn was grasped in handfuls and cut, or rather sawed, by the serrated edge of the sickle. Here the stubble was left long and was harrowed during the frosts of winter when it was brittle. The loose straw was then gathered with rakes and used for litter. With Mary Ann tying the sheaves, William was able to harvest one acre a day and he reckoned that the seven shillings they earned every day would go a long way to see them through the following winter. If that winter was a severe one, freezing the top twelve inches of clayland, William knew deep down that he would be out of a job draining the fields. So he thought it good policy to work sweating in the harvest field and put by some sovereigns, not for a rainy day, but for a freezing winter.

William's tools were primitive and simple. With the right hand he swung as large a bagging hook as money could buy. The bagging hook with a knife edge was much heavier than the sickle with the saw edge, used by the women. With his bagging hook William cut the wheat close to the ground, harvesting plenty of straw for thatching and bedding down the yarded cattle. The pickthank, a wooden crook, was held in the left hand and used to collect the cut corn into sheaves. William's pickthank was made of ash wood.

I often handled this rough crook, or wooden hook, when it hung from a nail in our wash-house. Daddocky we called it owing to the age-old decay in the wood, and how it escaped the fireplace for so long I sometimes wondered. Mary Ann carried no tools but gathered the sheaves together with her bare hands. Each sheaf she bound with a straw bond, which she made from the cut corn, and tied it with a special knot.

What a beautiful sight in the harvest field as William and Spider, bending low with their hooks, the metal shining in the sun as the blade cut the corn within six inches of the ground, the heavy heads of wheat falling in a graceful form before being hooked into sheaves by the pickthank. They cut, and the women tied, until the mid-day sun baked the cornfield, making the standing wheat crackle and the reapers hunger and thirst for food and drink. But the picture left to me, a word picture, by Uncle Jim, shows the toil and backache of the mid-nineteenth century harvest field. Breaks in the work were few, for if long rests were made in the heat of the day the target of an acre cut, tied and stooked, would not be reached. In fact, if the August thunder storm laid the corn it became difficult to cut three-quarters of an acre a day. William could not read or write, but he knew by a sort of intuition how many yard paces it took either way to add up to an acre of corn cut. It was vital for him to have cut, and Mary Ann to have tied, well over half an acre by dinner time. The sheaves had to be stooked up in stooks of eight before nightfall, and the stooking was shared by the men with the hooks and the women who tied the sheaves at the twilight hour.

By ten o'clock in the morning William and Mary Ann would be ready for a drink. As William quaffed the cider from his costrel barrel, Mary Ann sipped cold tea from her bottle. A crust of bread and cheese, with perhaps an onion, was eaten as they stood, as if on some hurried march.

Spider was what Uncle Jim called sweethearting Millie, the daughter of Walter Peart, the Squire's shepherd from Somerset. At dinner time, when Mary Ann and Millie fetched the frail baskets belonging to their men from the shade of the hedge, they all four sat together and ate the cold fat bacon and drank from their costrels and bottles. William would take off his heavy flannel shirt soaked with sweat and spread it over a stook of corn to dry in the sun.

Every dinner time when the food and drink had been taken, Millie Peart gave Spider a certain look. William knew what that look meant. Mary Ann knew what it meant. Millie wanted Spider to take her under the shade of the hedgerow oak. Before she would start the afternoon work Spider had to make love to her. Spider didn't mind, and obliged every day in the harvest field.

"We be getting married at Christmas," she told Mary Ann when Mary asked her what she would do if Spider got her in the family way. "Be you in the family way, Mary?" Millie asked.

"Ay, come next February, William and me hope to have a youngster in the house," Mary replied, but again warned Millie about her and Spider doing the last job first. It's true, Spider did marry Millie the following Christmas, and she wasn't far behind Mary Ann having her first baby.

When the Squire's corn was cut and stooked and stood like aisles of cathedrals in long rows on the yellow golden stubble, Alf Stubbs once more greased the axles and the guides on Baldwyn's waggons. The blue and red, and yellow and red four-wheeled carriers of corn and hay were housed in the thatched cart hovels at the Manor. On wet days after the haymaking, little boys with bone-handled shut knives, ferreted out the green shoots from grass seeds which had sprouted up in the cracks between the boards which made up the bed of the waggons. This growing grass, if it were left there, would soon cause decay.

Alf Stubbs was helped by Jim Dance, that man of so many parts from the nag stables. Between them they put the wooden grease jack under the waggon axles, knocked out the chisel-shaped cotter pin which held the wheels, removing the wheels, then plastered the axles with thick yellow cart grease. The Squire could not bear to hear a squeaking or the noise of the dry guides when the shaft horse turned the waggon wheels.

The staddles stood with the timbers and faggots as a foundation over the mushroom-shaped staddle stones. Before the first load came into the rickyard these staddles were covered with dry straw from last year's harvest. Walter Peart was told to build the ricks on these foundations, which stood eighteen inches above the rickyard, high and dry, safe from damp, safe from rats and mice. Fred Dunn, Jim Dance and Long Fred unloaded the waggons and served Walter at the rick.

Neal, Dan, Spider and William pitched and loaded in the harvest field, while Alf Stubbs the carter went to and fro with loaded waggons from the fields to the rickyard. He used two horses to pull the loads of corn up the steep, rough road to the rickyard. A lad who lodged with Fred Dunn met Alf halfway in the Groaten road with two more horses and the empty waggon.

William and Spider pitched the sheaves to Neal and Dan on the waggon with the ears of corn pointing to the middle of the load, and the loaders loaded what is known as boat fashion, that is the sheaves were higher at the fore and hind end of the waggon than in the middle. This made it easier for the pitchers and the middle would be loaded last of all.

Walter in the rickyard was careful to build a decent roof on his ricks. Some ricks were rectangular while others were round at the base. Walter's job after harvest would be to thatch the ricks in the evenings when he had finished shepherding for the day.

The oats were left in the field until last in case there was some moisture in the sheaves or green ears, as the Squire was particular that the threshed oats would not be mouldy or heated when Jim Dance fed them to his hunters. So they observed the old maxim that oats should hear the bells ring in the village church before they are ricked.

Uncle Jim recalled William's stories of the last load hauled from the fields into Squire Baldwyn's rickyard. The whole village was in the field as women and children raised their voices in the shout of "Harvest Home". On the last waggon Alf Stubbs hooked the best horses in the Squire's team. On the foremost horse was seated a beautiful girl, her straw bonnet decorated with a wreath of flowers. The horses were decked in the same way; each one was led by one of the Squire's men browned with summer toil. Other children rode on the loaded waggons, cheering, while one held a few of the finest ears upon the tines of a pitchfork. These ears were decorated with coloured ribbons in the evening and suspended from a beam in the barn where the harvest home was held.

Henry Baldwyn stood at the gate of the Manor with a foaming tankard of ale in his hand to welcome another harvest. Beside him stood his wife and son, the young Squire William.

The villagers, young and old, sang a song nearly as old as Bredon Hill. Tilda Dance's high-pitched nightingale voice was way above the rest, that voice which was still talked of when I was a boy seventy years later.

> Summer's toiling now is past;
> Harvest now hath sent her last —
> Her last, last, load,
> If the field containeth more,
> Master, give it to the poor!
> Abroad — Abroad,
> Let them through the corn fields roam,
> While we welcome harvest home —
> Harvest home, Harvest home,
> While we welcome harvest home;
> Songs shall sound and ale cups foam
> While we welcome harvest home.

In the great thatched barn, where the cider barrels stood under the wall facing the double doors like black

76

sleeping pigs, the harvest home supper was prepared. The barrels, now mostly empty, were rolled to one side all except the ten-hogshead cask which was too heavy to move.

Men arrived in clean white smocks, their faces ruddy with toil and health. Seats were arranged around the trestle tables while at the end of the table, spaces were reserved for the Squire's family. The old Squire carved a sirloin of beef, while his wife and servants were busy loading the plates of his men and their wives. Enormous plum puddings steamed from the serving table; Jim Dance drew jugs of cider from a barrel of the best.

William had Mary Ann's company for the first time at a harvest supper. Spider sat opposite Millie. She had bound up his sheaves all through the harvest and when any thorns or thistles pierced her fingers, he had extracted them so carefully. They had sat down on the same sheaf together and Spider had made love to her. Ah, he thought, come Christmas, the Squire has promised me a cottage, and we'll marry.

Old stories were told, old songs were sung. The village orchestra played on their violins, flutes, drums, fifes, while Long Fred played the big bass viol. Among the candles, the cider tots and the empty plates, the Squire sat supreme at the top of the table with Archdeacon Timbrell at one side and Mrs. Baldwyn on the other. The harvest home was over again for the old man whose ancestors had been growing corn here for five hundred years. It only remained for a toast to be given to Mr. and Mrs. Baldwyn by Jim Dance.

It ran as follows:

Now supper is over and all things are past
Here's our Mistress's good health in a full
    flowing glass,
She is a good Mistress she provides us good
    cheer,
Here's our Mistress's good health, boys, come
    drink up our beer.
Here's health to our Master, the Lord of the feast.
God bless his endeavours and give him increase
And send him good crops that we may meet
    another year.
Here's our Master's good health, boys, come
    drink up our beer.

It was now the turn of the gleaners to gather the loose ears in the fields. What a sight it was to see the women gleaning with their children. Little things, these children, with hard red legs shining amongst the stubble, stooping now and then to pick up an ear of corn, or raising their little heads to scare away a crow, or standing with their scissors to clip off the long straw and put the ears of corn into the bags which their mothers had tied on them. Those in the village who had no holding of their own to harvest were glad of the gleanings done by their wives and children. A family could glean enough wheat to thresh four bushels, which would keep them in bread for quite a while. In Gloucestershire, in this area, this was known not as gleaning, but as leasing.

I love gleaning for Ruth's sake, when I think of Ruth gleaning in the field of Boaz and her kindness to Naomi while she longed for the plains of Moab. Then Ruth was invited to sit down with the reapers and eat and drink with them and Boaz told the reapers to let Ruth glean among the sheaves before the corn was carried. When Boaz ordered his men to let some handfuls of corn fall on purpose for her so that she might glean more for herself and Naomi, it followed that Ruth became the wife of Boaz and Naomi, who was so poor, sold her land to him.

When the harvest was safely ricked, William borrowed a waggon from the Squire and with Spider's help he carried his sheaves off his acre of wheat in Carrants Field and ricked them in a little round rick near the pigsty at the back of his house. His acre was ample to supply flour for the bread oven for a whole year.

My grandmother, Mary Ann, used to remember her first harvest with William before she started a family, and when she spoke of it, the hardships and backaches of those days were forgotten.

CHAPTER
TEN

West of Bredon

The estate at Merecombe on the western side of Bredon Hill was owned by Squire Hopton Parsons whose land adjoined the Baldwyn estate. It was his family who had built the Folly on Bredon summit. Mr. Parsons was a great sporting character who enjoyed hunting on the Hill from Merecombe, where he ran a pack of beagles that had been bred selectively from some of the finest animals in this part of the country. Stories of his hospitality, his parties, his hare hunts and his shoots were the talk of the village around the Hill, and beyond.

A frequent visitor at Merecombe was Hopton Parsons' nephew, George, who lived on an estate between the Forest of Dean and the valley of the River Wye, and wrote to his uncle from Cromer where he had been campaigning in the Yarmouth election. But his affections are clearly some counties to the west.

Cromer August 8th

Dear Sir,

It's quite an age since I have had the pleasure of hearing from you. I have no person to blame but

80

myself. I did receive a letter from you when I was in Town; you can imagine that is the last place that a man can sit down and write.

I came to Cromer after my campaign at Yarmouth which was vastly pleasant and I am quite sorry to return to the solitary mansion.

I find that scarlet is the only colour to attract the females and had I remained much longer you would have heard of me conveying a sea nymph to Gretna Green.

I think with much pleasure of seeing you in November. I shall have killed all the partridges and pheasants in the County by that time.

I look forward to my visit to Gloucestershire and expect to find wonderful alterations. Have you had any good parties lately? I wish I could surprise you one Wednesday and shake your hand just as you are entering into the chair with our friend John Darke.

In your last letter you asked are you still mounted. I could answer yes; tolerably, but what may happen between now and November I can't tell.

What a disappointment for father from Clearwell that Clarinet could not start at Tetbury. I'm afraid he can't stand training; a subject I speak feelingly upon.

I am your dutiful nephew,
George Wyndham.

At the same time Hopton Parsons received a letter in a more anxious vein from George Bass, the tenant farmer at Beckford who had been so keen for Squire Wakeman to buy a threshing machine. George Bass had shot a hare on Hopton Parson's estate. It so happened that Bass was leaving Beckford to rent a farm off Lord Tyrconnel on his other estate in South Gloucestershire, so he was terribly worried that a report of his shooting might be sent from Merecombe to the Earl. George Bass said how sorry he was to kill the hare but his spaniel found it in the ley and it was the only hare he had seen in seven years there.

It appeared that Hopton Parsons now owned the land farmed by George Bass and retained the shooting rights. "I have no desire to break in upon your privacy," George wrote. He signed himself, "your most obedient yet unworthy servant. G. Bass". He added that he would like to keep the hare for his friends. The Squire of Merecombe accepted the apology and recommended him as a suitable tenant for the Earl.

So George Bass left Beckford and took with him his implements, harrows, ploughs, carts, waggons, ladders, hurdles in a convoy of horses and vehicles through Tewkesbury and Gloucester to the Berkeley Vale. Mrs. Bass had no children and was a delicate woman so George was pleased to become a tenant on the Earl's estate near Berkeley. It was much nearer to Bath than Beckford and Mrs. Bass had benefited by visiting that spa for her ailments. In fact, George Bass was a martyr to rheumatism and he was fond of the spa waters.

George Bass became tenant to Tyndal Farm, not far from the historic Berkeley Castle. His farm at Beckford had been hilly, sheep country, thin, stony, not good milking land. But the Berkeley Vale grew lush grass and corn and potatoes, so he sold his Cotswold ewes at Gloucester Barton Fair, and took his Shorthorn cows with him, for he had been experienced in dairy farming.

Before her marriage, Mrs. Ada Bass worked for Squire Wakeman in his dairy, making the butter and cheese. She became well known as his finest cheese maker. Mr. Wakeman's cows grazed the Carrant Brook meadows, a herd of the old Gloucester breed which Sam Tombs, his bailiff, had built up from three heifers and a bull he bought for the Squire at Gloucester Market. The familiar golden-coloured Double Gloucester cheese from the Wakeman vats and press was sold to the retired army officers and their families in Cheltenham. Ada did her best to make a good cheese from her husband's Shorthorns off the Hill, and George sold it at a few pence per pound in Tewkesbury. Now Ada was keen for George to use Gloucester cattle for the Berkeley dairy.

Though the land was richer, George Bass found the buildings at Tyndal Farm to be poor compared with Beckford, though the house itself was spacious with a fireplace in the hall big enough to take a four-foot cord of wood. As George walked his riverside meadows that Michaelmas he noticed some of his neighbours still milking their cows in the field. "I don't know, Ada," he remarked. "It's a long way to carry the milk with a yoke and two buckets from the riverside to our dairy."

He rode his horse over to Sam Tombs, who had also left Beckford recently to become the Earl's bailiff. His house was on the higher land towards the Cotswold edge. "Dost like the Vale farm, George?" his farmer neighbour questioned.

"Ah, 'tis good pasture, good plough land, and a tidy house the Earl has rented me but the building be devilishly poor, made for dwarfs, I reckon, no yud room see. The cow shed be so low roofed."

"Now, George, what you want on that farm be some Gloucester cows, the mahogany coloured beasts like I had at Beckford."

"Just what the Missus says, Sam, but I don' relish milking down in the meadows which flood from the Severn."

"What about a cow shed and yard, George?" Sam asked.

George stood in the rick yard at the bailiff's farm while his horse munched hay in Sam's stable. He wondered whether it was wise to ask his landlord's bailiff for a building for his cows so soon after coming to the farm. He wasn't sure what the Earl's reaction would be, for he knew that other farmers would have liked the tenancy of Tyndal. There was no need for George Bass to answer the bailiff's question. Sam explained the Earl had suggested some while back that a reasonable cow shed was needed at Tyndal, and there was ample timber on the estate to make it. That following spring a timber-built and strawthatched building was erected, big enough to house fifteen cows at the manger. Ada was delighted to see the building so close to the dairy, the well and the pump. The Earl's estate workers made the manger from seasoned elm planks that had been sawn in the saw pit years before. The bottom of the manger was made of blue stone slabs, where the cows could eat their mangolds and swede turnips as if from a clean plate.

From a small herd of Gloucester cattle at a farm near Nailsworth, George Bass selected four cows in milk and in calf and he and Ada drove them to Berkeley.

Squire Hopton Parsons of Merecombe heard from Lord Tyrconnel that his new tenant, George Bass, was founding a herd of Gloucester cattle and he good-naturedly sent his man over to Ashton to enquire of Mr. Baldwyn if he knew where any of Mr. Wakeman's Gloucesters had been dispersed to. It happened that David Drinkwater of the Orchard Farm had bought some of the Wakeman stock and had bred a few young Gloucester cattle from some oldish cows from the Beckford herd.

"Drinkwater of Ashton has a young Gloucester bull in the orchard next to my cowman's house at the Croft," was the message Mr. Hopton Parsons' man brought home from Mr. Baldwyn. The message was sent to George Bass at Berkeley by the Bristol coach. With two horses and a bull float, George Bass came to Ashton and bought the bull off David Drinkwater, and it was in this way that George and Ada Bass founded the Gloucester dairy herd, which became more famous for the production of cheese than the Beckford herd of Mr. Wakeman.

"You must thank Mr. Hopton Parsons for finding us that bull," Ada said to her husband.

"I'll do more than that," George promised. He rode to Bristol and bought twelve flasks of some of the best oil he had tasted, a jar of capers, another of anchovies and put them on the Tewkesbury coach directed to Mr. H. Parsons of Merecombe. As for himself, the Squire was pleased that George Bass had established himself a suitable tenant for his friend, Lord Tyrconnel at Berkeley.

Sam Tombs, bailiff to the Earl, knew that the Hopton Parsons' estate was an excellent place to buy stock of all description. He asked for one hundred brace of carp to stock the Earl's large pool. "A wile boat will be at the house in the tree to receive them," he wrote to Merecombe. The Earl himself wrote to Hopton Parsons offering two young hounds, a very good little dog named Softwood and a bitch named Radical, taught to go as a couple, and an older hound named Launcelot. The Merecombe beagles had been having varying fortunes, but there was some good hunting in the Vale at Parmington.

I suppose Mr. Hopton Parsons was unique in a way, having a pack of beagles and also running another pack of harrier hounds, followed by the farmers and landowners of the Bredon Hill villages. It's usual for the hare to run in circles around the fields on the Bredon Hill plateau until March, when the jack hare will take a straight line. This February day, however, Hopton

Parsons' pack started a hare in Ashton Parish Quarry which, taking a line past the beeches by Great Hill barn, for he was undoubtedly a jack, made for the coppice at the north end of Ashton village. The hounds lost him and as night fell, the huntsman had the difficulty of calling all his hounds together to return to Merecombe. One dog hound was lost, spending the night roaming the village.

The following day was Sunday. Jim Dance, Mr. Baldwyn's groom, had a nice sirloin on the table ready for his Sunday dinner. Tilda left the kitchen for a while to fetch water from the well. She came back to find the meat had gone and saw a hound running with the joint down the garden. Jim wrote to Mr. Hopton Parsons:

Dear Sir,

On Sunday, the last day of February, a hound belonging to you came into my house and took from the table a joint of meat cooked for dinner. Sometime before a dog of yours killed three couple of ducks of mine.

I asked for a hare and you promised one but never gave me, though you presented them all over the neighbourhood and next door. You forgot your promise.

You ordered my dog to be shot for no trespass at all.

Pray, what must I do to your dog for trespassing on me?

Yours,
J. Dance.

The good Squire's answer to this uncompromising epistle is not recorded.

Back at Tyndal Farm, Berkeley, George Bass and Ada had a bad winter with their health. Ada, who was not too strong when she left Beckford, had been so much better at Berkeley until she developed the cough she wrote about to Hopton Parsons. A cough, which, she says, responded well to the treatment prescribed by a neighbour. Every day she drank a pint of ass's milk. George was away at Bath taking the cure for his rheumatics. She writes, "These waters do not show their effects for some time and George is staying until Christmas."

She had her brother living with her to help with the dairy and records that she had squeezed the apples for cider and took a dry cow to Gloucester Market and sent a short flitch of bacon, with the ham cut off, to George in Bath by the Bristol waggon.

Now, with George away at Bath, Ada was homesick for Beckford as she struggled with the farm in Berkeley Vale. She made better cheese there, it's true, but missed her friends around Bredon Hill. She even missed the stern Reverend Timbrell as he drove around the village in his coach; the closeness of friendly Hopton Parsons; the sight of William Archer and Spider draining the clay. She wondered how William and Mary Ann and Spider and Millie fared, and how the Methodists up Cottons Lane were and whether fourteen still attended and sang around the organ on Sunday nights. She wondered if William and Mary Ann still took the footpath to Merecombe some Sundays.

William and Mary Ann did still go to Merecombe where Mr. Mumford, a neighbouring landlord of Hopton Parsons, preached in the chapel on Sunday nights. He had built the chapel back in 1819, of stone with a blue slate roof where eighty-three members gathered. So William and Mary Ann still had strong ties with Merecombe where the building with the school room adjoining rang out on Sundays to Wesley's hymns and George Mumford's voice, west of Bredon.

CHAPTER
ELEVEN

A Michaelmas Flight

By the light of guttering tallow candles, and the glow of the hearth fire, Martha Dunn and Lotty Stubbs worked at evening in Fred Dunn's kitchen. They were plaiting straw, clean and bright from the harvest, to line horses' collars.

Fred Dunn and Alf Stubbs were at the kitchen table repairing the harness from the farm, working with needles, wax ends and leather thongs. When that was done, Alf intended to fix another sned in his scythe, while Fred was to put a new leather thong on the swingel of his flail. The scythe would not be used again that year, but soon the two men would be threshing with their flails; in fact they thrashed enough corn to provide seed for the autumn planting.

"I'll see Walter Peart in the morning," Alf said. "A fleece or two of wool I want to go in the hosses' collars when we send them to the saddler with the straw plait. Eases the horses' shoulders it do, dost know."

Martha and Lotty were gossiping about their neighbours, about how Walter and Fanny Peart had got a full house now with Spider moved in and married to their Millie and the youngster born in March and them only married last Christmas.

"Lucky fella, young Spider is, taking up with Millie," Alf remarked.

"Oi, hair as black as the raven's wing, wide in the hips, full in the bosom. Fine upstanding maid her was, well, still is now her's had a young 'un," was Fred's contribution.

Martha Dunn poked the fire, making the sparks from the dry hawthorn log shoot up the chimney like golden turd flies. She grabbed another wisp of straw. "To think that our husbands talk like that about Fanny Peart's daughter, and both of them old enough to be her father. You're not describing a brood mare, Fred Dunn. Wide in the hips, if you please . . ."

But the men only laughed gently. "We all saw young Spider sweethearting with her mid-day in the cornfield when he was harvesting with William Archer," Alf volunteered.

"Oi, he's a lucky fella, say what you like," Fred added. And the two men laughed and remembered.

At that moment the lucky fella himself arrived carrying two geese he had killed for Squire Baldwyn. "Yer, Master Baldwyn wants these two birds plucked for tomorrow. It's Michaelmas and he's invited his neighbours to a supper."

"No trouble at all, Spider," Lotty said. "And how's that youngster of yours. Henry, isn't it? After the Squire, I reckon."

Spider then told the two farm workers' wives to be careful to save the long flight feathers off the geese, and

91

off all the other geese he would be bringing for plucking. There seemed to be some sort of mystery attached to this order.

"Mind," he said, "Master Baldwyn says me and Millie can have the down feathers off the breast to stuff a mattress for our bed."

"You find a difference, I'll warrant, to sleeping on oat flights at Beckford when you worked for Master Wakeman," Alf suggested.

"Oi, oat flights from the threshing, a 'ooden bed which had to be scrubbed with vinegar every summer to keep away the bugs, and the bedding baked in the sun. Sam Tombs the bailiff was particular 'cos the cowman afore me wasn't keen on soap and water."

Spider left the women to their plaiting and the men to their harness mending, but Fred Dunn was more curious than the rest about what the flight feathers were needed for by Squire Baldwyn. "He don't want they there feathers for making quill pens, Alf, 'cos the birds be only three parts grown, an' not like they 'ull be come Christmas. The feathers 'ull make quills then."

This seemed a sensible comment from his friend, and Alf had little to add, just an under his breath mutter and grunt about the gentry eating geese at Michaelmas, three parts grown.

Martha and Lotty plucked the geese, preserving the flight feathers for Mr. Baldwyn and the down feathers for Spider.

The following evening Squire Baldwyn sent another two geese to be plucked by the women. Spider came with the news that a young fellow had come to live at

David Drinkwater's. "A real toff he be in his tweed breeches, Norfolk jacket and smokes a big cigar."

"Oh, that explains it," Lotty said to Martha. "The shirts I washed last week, they didn't look like David's. Made by a London firm, according to the label inside. Wonderful quality, Martha. Yes, beautiful shirts."

"You still do Mr. Drinkwater's washing then, Lotty?" Martha said.

Lotty then told Martha Dunn how David Drinkwater's mother had shown her how to wash clothes when she was working there as a girl of twelve years old and now David sent his farm boy down every Monday with the washing in a basket.

"You mean that boy Tilda Dance had afore she married Jim?" Martha remarked with a deep sigh.

"Now don't thee get speculating who fathered that un," was Alf's reply to that open question.

Spider wasn't interested in Lotty's washing or who was the father of Tilda Dance's boy, but he told the folk in Dunn's kitchen that the man living at Drinkwater's up Cottons Lane had come to learn farming. "Comes from a circus family, William Archer told me in the pub t'other night, but I must get on 'cos Master Timbrell has got a Vestry Meeting tonight and being clerk, I must be there."

"Clerk," Fred Dunn taunted. "What bist gwain to be next, you? Be a cut above we chaps now, Spider, and they tells me you have started pig killing. Butcher now, ay?"

"Oi, I be killing one for William Archer in the morning at six o'clock. Jim Dance and that boy of

Tilda's as went away and now works for David, are gwain to help hold him."

Next morning Spider arrived at William Archer's house when it was just getting light. The pig, starved of food for twelve hours, was looking over the sty door. William had two boltings of dry straw ready to burn off the bristles; Mary Ann had the copper boiler full of hot water to clean the pig.

Jim Dance walked up the road carrying a four-legged pig bench. Young Joe Salter was by his side carrying a broom. They put the bench and broom on the gravel path in William's garden.

"Fairish pig," Jim commented. "Sixteen score, I'll warrant."

"Oi," William replied, "'twas fed in the main from Carrants Field. Taters, cabbage, parsnips and tail corn, besides what the Missus put in the pig wash barrel; all the waste from the table."

"Well done, young William," Jim said, "but there is a bit of that pig Squire Baldwyn and David Drinkwater would like."

"They be welcome to a bit of spare-rib or griskin, to be sure they be."

"They want the pig's bladder and the bladder out of every pig you kill, Spider," was Jim's unexpected reply.

"Hell's bells, what the nation for?" the young butcher said. "What's going on in the parish? First I'm collecting goose feathers, now pigs' bladders. Now bladders, when they beun't used for storing the lard in, make toys for youngsters to blow up, but what David

94

and the Squire are collecting them for I udn't care to gamble. Uvout they be making a fool on ma."

"You take the bladder to the Manor, Jim, and I'm asking no questions; but had the Squire wanted a bit of meat he would have been welcome, wouldn't he, Mary?" William said, turning to Mary Ann who was stoking the boiler. "Let's get this bit of a job done, Spider. I must get back to the rick thatching by seven o'clock."

Spider killed the pig on the bench, burned off its bristles with a bolting of straw, then scrubbed the rend or sward with hot water, then cold, until the Gloucester Old Spot pig was as white as snow. The liver and the pluck chitterlings were put on Mary's kitchen table, then the open pig was hung in William's stable to cool and set, but not before the carcass had been weighed on Jim Dance's steelyard scales.

"As near as damn it to sixteen score," Spider said as he returned to Mr. Baldwyn's farmyard with Jim, Joe Salter and the pig's bladder. In the dairy several pigs' bladders hung from the beams drying like parchment.

As William thatched the corn ricks around Tythe Court, he felt relieved that his pig, which he had fed for nine months, would now be helping to feed him and Mary Ann.

At that moment the Squire himself came to the rickyard. "Spider has killed your pig, William, and I understand it was sixteen score weight." Mr. Baldwyn's remark caused Grandfather to hang on to the ladder and drop a little straw from his hand. "Yes, sir," he

95

replied, "a useful pig and when the flitches are cured they will make two good pictures in our house. But," curiosity overcame him, "why, sir, did you want the bladder, if I might enquire?"

"Just a fad. Just a fad. Nothing particular."

"You know, sir," William continued, "that you would have been very welcome to a bit of the best meat."

"That's all right, William," was the Squire's answer. "Spider is killing one for me tomorrow."

William was thatching the tallest rick in the rickyard, circular at the base on staddle stones, raised on a wooden and faggot foundation above the damp floor of the rickyard and away from the rats and mice. The ricks were built in a rough circle around the outside of the yard. The middle formed an amphitheatre where the straw for thatching was drawn into neat boltings ready for water-proofing the rick roofs. It was here that the withey branches were split into rick pegs for holding on the straw thatch.

William made straw ropes with his scud winder, a kind of brace with a hook on the end to wind the straw. These ropes he used to tie on the thatch. Standing in this arena he saw little of the outside world, just ricks, and more ricks encircling him.

The following Sunday afternoon William, Mary Ann and baby Phoebe walked up the Cottons Lane with Spider, Millie and baby Henry. When they got as far as David Drinkwater's orchard they were surprised to see, turned out with his horses, two beautiful skewbald ponies grazing.

"Belongs to that fella," Spider suggested. "I know he's from a circus. Young Joe Salter says he can crack a whip accurate enough to cut a gnat's eye out."

"What's his name?" William asked.

"Alfredo summat, wasn't it, Millie, what Joe told us."

Spider was dubious about this chap coming here and he told the others that "it wouldn't be for the good".

Joe Salter and Alfredo every morning saddled the two ponies while Alfredo rode in a circle in Drinkwater's orchard. He rode jumping tree stumps. He rode with blindfolds on. Then one day he lit a fire and jumped his pony through the fire. The smaller of the two ponies he jumped through the hoops of a cider barrel. "Practising for summat, I reckon," Alf Stubbs said.

"Comes from Italy he told me in the pub, but he speaks passable English," Fred Dunn said.

"It's quite a show, days now, up at Drinkwater's," Spider told William as he talked over the gate one Sunday after church and chapel.

On Sunday nights when Spider had been to church and Grandfather to chapel, the Watchets and the Archers got together for a couple of hours. Walter and Fanny Peart looked after young Henry, allowing their daughter and son-in-law to go along to William and Mary's house. Around the fire William and Spider drank the cider from William's barrel in crock mugs, or tots as they called them, while Mary Ann and Millie sipped tea and exchanged tales about their babies.

It seemed that Spider was always first with the news. Working as he did almost under the Squire's window, along in the cattle pens, he was bound to hear things. "Some sort of a show or circus the Squire and David Drinkwater are arranging. It wasn't mentioned at the Vestry Meeting but I overheard them talking about it afterwards. Alfredo is at the back of it. He's gwain to ride the skewbald ponies."

"That's as might be, Spider, but I've got further news." William burst out laughing as he said this and Mary Ann put her tea cup down and tried to remain sedate.

"An Italian girl is coming on the Tewkesbury coach in a day or two. 'Tis Alfredo's sweetheart."

"But where's she going to stay? At Mr. Drinkwater's?" Millie exclaimed.

"No," William replied. "Mr. Baldwyn has asked Fred Dunn if he will board and mess her for a fortnight. Martha's damn near off her head about it 'cos you know how Fred Dunn is partial to the ladies."

The whole conversation that Sunday was on the forthcoming show, whatever it was to be.

Some days after, David Drinkwater got the message that the lady was arriving at Tewkesbury at mid-day. Joe Salter was sent with Alfredo and the horse and trap to bring her to Ashton. All eyes were on the party as David Drinkwater's horse trotted the trap up the village and the lady alighted at the Dunns' cottage. Alfredo acted as interpreter to his girlfriend, explaining that her name was Teresa and she spoke little English.

Alf and Lotty Stubbs came to the Dunns' cottage that first night. The men laughed and winked at each other, while the women remained serious and quiet.

"All right to laugh, Fred," Martha said to him as they went to bed after Teresa had been seen to her room. "Yes, all right for you and Alf to laugh, but how would you like an Italian man here with me for a fortnight?"

"How didst get on along 'uv the Italian wench last night, you?" Fred Dunn was greeted with this question by Alf the morning after Teresa's arrival in the village.

"Ah, don't mention it, 'cos my life's a gwain to be stormy at home now we got her under the roof," Fred replied with a sigh.

But the Dunns saw little of Teresa during the day when she trained in Drinkwater's orchard with Alfredo, ready for the forthcoming show. What exactly David Drinkwater and the Squire intended putting on no one seemed to know. One thing was certain, Alfredo and Teresa were going to perform with the skewbald ponies.

"Beautiful clothes she has got. A real leopard skin jacket and jewellery," Martha confided to Lotty.

A week before Hallowe'en, posters printed by a Tewkesbury printer appeared in the Star Inn, outside the Manor, at Drinkwater's orchard and one in the church porch, announcing the programme for a show on the eve of All Souls, October 31st, at the Manor by kind permission of Squire Henry Baldwyn with David Drinkwater as Master of Ceremonies. Top of the bill gave every villager a surprise. It was something unimaginable.

1. Alfredo, star of the great Italian circus, will attempt to fly from the top of Mr. Baldwyn's highest corn rick.

2. Teresa of Naples, that fearless horsewoman, will ride a pony through the hoops of a hogshead barrel. She will ride around the ring standing on two ponies.
   She will attempt her dare devil act of jumping through blazing straw.
3. Alfredo will ride and jump a thatched shepherd's hurdle with Teresa on his shoulders.
4. An open contest of shin kicking when William Archer, champion of Bredon Hill, takes on all comers for a belt.
5. A welcome to Ivan and his dancing bear.
6. Selections from Ashton Church Band conducted by Mr. Watchet.
7. A sparrow shoot from traps in Ten Furlong.
8. A supper in Mr. Baldwyn's barn for all villagers over thirteen years of age.

"A rum how do you do, this show at Hallowe'en," Walter said to Long Fred in the Star Inn. "Alfredo's a gwain to fly off a corn rick. I go to Hell if he won't break his neck. Now what dost thee think of this caper, Fred?"

Long Fred, who was a man of few words, nodded, lit his pipe, spat, hit the spittoon and muttered, "If he damn well breaks his neck it 'ull be one less for us to keep 'cos he's come yer being foolhardy and don't go to work like thee and me. No, I shan't loose no sleep over him. No, Walter." But Long Fred had more words to say for, at that moment, William Archer and Spider Watchet came into the Star kitchen. "Thee bist a close sort a cratur, William, not telling us that thurs shin kicking at the show."

William told Long Fred that, "'Twas only yesterday that David told me about my part in the show and told Spider to bring the orchestra along."

Martha agreed to find a home for Teresa until after the show, but then she would have to go. Jim and Tilda Dance were asked to attend to the catering and the supper in the barn.

On the morning of the big day William Archer and Spider Watchet were busy on the Squire's instructions, spreading a mat of straw on the rickyard floor near the big rick where Alfredo was expected to land. The ricks, now all neatly thatched by William, formed a ring, almost like a circus ring. Under the supervision of David Drinkwater a staging had been erected against a rick opposite the tallest one, from which Alfred was to attempt his flight. It was a great day for the village. Hopton Parsons, Squire of Merecombe, came over to open the show. "A fine job you have made, Henry, organising your yard, and paddock and buildings for this event," he said.

Mr. Parsons' wife, Henry Baldwyn, Archdeacon Timbrell, Mrs. Baldwyn and David Drinkwater sat on a bench while the Squire of Merecombe said a few words to open the show. When he sat down, David Drinkwater rose and with the clarion voice of a showman announced the start of proceedings. Not since the road had been re-made from Hinton Cross to the Tibblestone, he said, had there been a celebration.

"We have waited a long time for the new road to be finished. You remember how some years back Carrants Brook was flooded and the water gushed across the Naits, swilling away some of the hard work put in by our men. Well, our Squire has cleared out the brook, and my foreman George Archer there, has, with others, finished our road. So Mr. Baldwyn and myself thought it a good time to celebrate, and I am pleased to see some of the workers present, including George Archer, who was my assistant, and Archdeacon Timbrell tells me he can journey to Cheltenham in forty minutes in his coach and pair. That's a great improvement."

Archdeacon Timbrell then spoke for a few minutes, saying how pleased he was to be with his parishioners on this joyful occasion. "You may well be puzzled regarding the first item on this afternoon's programme. I am amazed at Alfredo's daring. As I read my Bible it says 'ye shall mount up with wings as eagles'. But you must not think that prophesy is being fulfilled in a literal sense." Then the Archdeacon took his seat as Spider Watchet led Alfredo into the ring.

He was dressed in tights and a red waistcoat and bright yellow shirt. His arms were like the wings of some great bird. They were dressed in goose feathers. His legs too were covered in feathers as far as his ankles. Around his waist were the pigs' bladders which Spider had saved from his butchering. Blown up, they were as big as mangold wurzels. Alfredo bowed and waved to the circle of village folk, then he saluted the gentlemen and ladies on the platform. The Squire's forty-rung ladder stood against the roof of the corn rick, where Grandfather was posted to give Alfredo the send off.

"Bist come to see that 'Talion break his neck, you?" Long Fred said to Walter Peart as they stood together with their backs against another rick.

"No, not exactly, but the feast in the big barn will be acceptable," he answered.

The village band or church orchestra played as Alfredo mounted the ladder. They played as he stood ready by William Archer's side. Then the music stopped, the crowd was silent, as the autumn breeze fluttered the wings of goose feathers and sent the blown up bladders bobbing up and down from Alfredo's waist. David Drinkwater called to the top of the rick, "We are ready." William Archer stood behind the Italian and supported his outstretched winged arms to help him get what benefit he could from the wind.

Alfredo jumped. He kept his arms outstretched like a gliding sea-gull. Ever so gently he came down with the bladders above his waist, and landed on the straw. He had flown across the rickyard. As he lay there winded, Spider ran and pulled him to his feet, and the crowd cheered. Alfredo had flown on goose's wings and pigs' bladders.

"Who is the fella stood by the pigsties with a note book?" Millie Peart asked Mary Ann.

"Don't know, I'm sure," she answered, "but perhaps Tilda Dance knows."

Tilda did know because he had stabled his horse in Jim Dance's stable and had ridden over from Worcester to put a report in *The Weekly Journal*. The rest of the programme was exciting, too. Teresa and Alfredo now rode the ponies, dare devil rides through fire and hoops. The sparrow shoot attracted the small farmers with their guns from around Bredon Hill. Sam Tombs came up from the Berkeley Vale and won the contest.

"Allus likes to see the sparrow shoot," Fred Dunn said to Alf Stubbs while they watched Teresa doing her last act on Alfredo's shoulders as he rode a skewbald pony.

"Oi, it makes it worthwhile going out at night and catching the birds out of the hedges like me and young Joe Salter have done with a bird batting net the last few nights," Alf answered, then added, "How many more nights is Teresa staying at your place, Fred? Has her taught you Italian yet or does the Missus allow you to talk to her, but then, I saw you giving her cider t'other evening by the shed."

"For Lord's sake, thee shut up, Alf. I've told ya before the trouble I've had with Martha." Fred hesitated a bit then said, "I'll tell tha all about it one day when the dust has settled. Her's a lovable wench." Alf laughed and speculated, but said nothing to cause trouble.

As the villagers watched Ivan the Russian dancing with his bear and the daylight gave way to twilight, Jim Dance rang a bell at the barn door as a signal that supper was ready. Tilda, Millie, Mary Ann and the other wives of the Squire's men had prepared a splendid feast.

When the food and drink was cleared from the trestle tables families sat around on boltings of straw in the great barn and drank cider listening with pleasure to Spider Watchet's orchestra playing their pieces, and watching Ivan and his dancing bear.

So ended a day to remember, a day when the folk of Ashton celebrated the end of the roadmaking to Tibblestone.

CHAPTER
TWELVE

A Funny Sort of Pig

After the show at Ashton, Ivan the Russian did a tour of the Bredon Hill villages dancing with his bear, doing his act at the Queen Elizabeth Inn at Elmley and the Fox and Hounds at Bredon. It was a little respite for the workers on the land in a dull foggy November to drink their ale and watch Ivan dance with his bear to tunes played by some village fiddler.

Ivan's problem was staying overnight in the villages with his bear. There would be accommodation in the inn for him, but what of the bear? It meant that they spent cold nights together in the stable of the inn or in some farmer's barn.

He came back to Ashton and danced, first of all at the Star then at the White Hart at the top of the village. "I have nowhere to stay tonight, William," he said to my grandfather.

"Welcome as the flowers in May you would be at our house if you hadn't got that bear, but with him and our little un, Phoebe, well, Mary Ann wouldn't allow you in our kitchen."

"Your stable, William. Could I stay in there tonight?"

William was sorry he could not be more helpful, but answered, "No. I've bought a donkey for fifteen shillings to help me with the work on Carrants Field. The donkey sleeps in there."

It was late in the evening and the landlord of the White Hart was ready for bed. William and Ivan each drank another pint of beer and then a thought came to Grandfather. "I don't like to offer it to you, but my pig sty is empty now Spider has killed my pig. There's straw in there and you can take the bear into the sty and bed down for the night, but I'm real sorry that it's the best I can offer."

Ivan, putting his hand on William's shoulder, said, "That will be excellent. I'll sleep there."

At William's house, near the White Hart, Mary Ann was worried about where her husband had been until so late. Standing at the back door with a candle in her hand she imagined she saw something shambling up the path. Her imagination proved to be true when a bear on a chain and the Russian came into the light of the candle. "What on earth have you brought back from the pub, Will? What ever next?" she said to her husband.

"'Tis all right, missus. Ivan's gwain to sleep in the sty tonight with the bear. Have you wound up the clock, Mary, 'cos I know it's gone nine o'clock?"

"Yes, I have and come on in and let's get to bed. You'll be late in the morning," she replied.

Ivan settled down on the straw in William's pigsty. After a night in the White Hart sleep was just a matter of lying down for the Russian. William had told him that "beer on top of cider is not a good rider" — an old saying, but true.

Mary Ann was wakeful, thinking of the man in the sty on a cold night. She nudged William several times when she heard the clank of the bear chain as the animal moved about. He was tied on the door post of the sty and could reach the little walled-in yard outside the door. "William," she said, "do you think the bear may slip his collar and get away, and have you locked the back door and put the bar up?"

William just muttered, "'Tis all right, my wench," and slept on.

It was one of those nights when the moon came over the Cotswold hills as big as a waggon wheel and lit the Vale so that every tree and house could be seen from the Archers' window. Just after William's grandfather clock struck two the sounds of wheels on the road outside and the clip clopping of a horse was heard. "Someone about, William," Mary Ann said. "A cart has stopped by our gate. Get up."

William just replied, "'Tis all right, I tell ya."

Mary Ann sat up in bed as the moonlight lit the room. She heard the clink of the iron garden gate and from the window saw clearly the shape of two men. The first man carried an empty sack bag. He went into the yard of the pigsty and the bear, ready for a dance, threw his front legs around the stranger's waist and hugged him closely to his bristly chest. The man screamed and tried to break loose and the bear growled like an angry dog.

William was now at the bedroom window and soon realised what the men had come for. "They be come to steal pig, Mary. Let 'um be and let the bear frighten 'um." The other man grabbed William's pitchfork and leaning over the wall poked at the bear who retreated into the sty. When Ivan came out from his drink-induced sleep, the two men fled to their horse and cart and cantered off towards Elmley.

When daylight came next day Mary Ann and William gave Ivan breakfast before he went on his way. William said that he had heard of quite a lot of pig stealing going on around Bredon Hill but he thought the culprits came from far away. They stole pigs, sold them, then moved on to another part of the country.

Grandfather and Spider Watchet were digging a drain up in the Dean the next day and spent the evening together with Fred Dunn, Alf Stubbs and Spider's Millie in the Archer cottage. While Millie and Mary Ann sat around the fire with their knitting, Spider, William, Fred Dunn and Alf Stubbs were out in the back kitchen drinking cider from William's barrel and smoking their clay pipes.

Fred who had been teased over the Italian girl, Teresa, now had a chance to pull William's leg. "Keeping a bear in the pigsty then William ay?" he said with a smile. "Hast got any cubs, yet awhile, you?"

"Oh, oi, but thee just wait til' I fly off a corn rick," he answered, puffing at his clay and holding a half full tot of cider in the other hand. "We be gwain into the circus business, that's right, 'unt it Spider?"

Spider was in a more serious mood for he had been talking to Archdeacon Timbrell after a Vestry Meeting. The Archdeacon, who was a local magistrate, said he would have liked to have entertained the two gentlemen in the trap who called at the Archers in Beckford Court House and given them a spell of hard labour. They could grind some Cotswold barley on Northleach treadmill. "'Tis like this, Fred," Spider said, "if William's pig had still been in the sty last night those varmints in the trap would have stolen it like they did at Merecombe."

"What happened there then, t'other side of the Hill?" Fred enquired.

Spider then told them the sorry tale he had heard from the Archdeacon about the misfortune of George Mumford, the Merecombe Methodist, whose chapel William and Mary Ann had sometimes attended. George Mumford was widely known as the most upright and God-fearing man around the Hill. Even the Archdeacon, who had no time for Methody preachers, spoke highly of him, and now he had lost a sow and a litter of ten. "He had just weaned them at eight weeks old," Spider explained. "Doing well on the barley meal, and the gentlemen in the trap, I suppose it was them, took the lot."

William Archer listened to Spider's melancholy tale, filled the cider mugs again, and invited his friends around the fire in the sitting room. "Phoebe gone to bed?" he asked his wife.

"Bless the fella, yes, 'tis eight o'clock," she replied.

Fanny Peart was looking after young Henry Watchet that evening, so that Millie could spend the time with her friend Mary Ann.

"Now, Fred," William began, "tell us about you and Teresa. Lucky chap you were to have her company and all I get is a dancing bear. You did promise to give us the story one day."

Fred Dunn's cheeks went redder and redder and it wasn't the cider that caused it. He shuffled his hob-nailed boots on the stone flag floor under the settle. He loosened the red spotted handkerchief from around his neck, stroked back his greying hair and answered, "William, that un't hadly jonnuck in front of the women folk 'cos if it gets back to Martha there 'ull be Hell to pay."

"Got something to hide then, have you, Fred?" Millie said with a laugh.

"No. Nothing out of place happened, but somehow she took a liking to me. Don't know why, mind, but she liked a drop of cider. Got her down one night it did in the hovel and I carried her upstairs and put her to bed."

"Oh, tell us more," Mary Ann cried.

"Nothing out of place happened, I said," Fred continued. "Like a child she lay in my arms up our little stairway and when I got her in bed she held my arm above the elbow and said, 'You strong man, I love you'."

"Have another tot of cider, Fred," William suggested when he stopped to recall more of that night, "and where was Martha that evening?"

"Gone with Lotty to take David Drinkwater's clean washing back up Cottons Lane, then she went back with Joe Salter, Tilda's boy, to Jim and Tilda Dance's."

Spider who had been morose that evening was loth to say anything in front of Millie and Mary Ann but plucked up courage to ask the burning question. "What did you do when she said that, Fred?"

"Hell for leather I went downstairs," he replied.

"I'll believe ya, but thurs thousands as wouldn't," Alf Stubbs said with a chuckle.

"Now be ya all satisfied?" Fred said.

The grandfather clock struck nine and William pulled the long chain until the heavy weight was up near the face, and opened the front door with his usual farewell, "Good night. I'm off to bed."

CHAPTER
THIRTEEN

Drunken Wills and Black Tauntons

My grandfather was so pleased with the donkey he had bought for fifteen shillings that he soon bought a cart and harness to complete the turn out. The land at Carrants Field, apart from the strawberry and gooseberry patch, was usually ploughed by Alf Stubbs, but after crops of peas and beans William would get enough mould or tilth to plant his wheat crop by breast ploughing. He had found Ned the donkey useful for taking produce to Evesham, but now there was another task he put him to. It had occurred to William that his donkey was always grazing the grass verges of Gypsies Lane while he was pushing the breast plough. I'll odds that, he thought, and we will share the work.

The breast plough blade skimmed the top two inches of the land, or a little deeper, if the ploughman lifted the long wooden handle and pitched the point of the share deeper into the soil. In this way William governed the depth of his work. I'll get deeper, he thought, if I hitch the donkey in front. William fixed a light chain just above the blade of the plough, put Ned in trace harness, hooking the traces to the chain with cord. Gee-oh lines, like Alf Stubbs used when ploughing with a pair of horses. You cried "Gee" to make the horse pull to the right, and "Oh" or "Aw" to pull to the left. In this way Grandfather was able to guide Ned the donkey, and the result was a primitive skim plough, before the one-horse skim was invented. With Ned's help William skimmed three inches deep in Carrants Field.

Squire Baldwyn was very good to Grandfather. He knew that this young stocky, broad-shouldered chap would thatch his ricks, cut his share of the corn, and mow the meadows with Spider, so when he asked for a week off to pick David Drinkwater's apples up Cottons Lane, his master only replied that he should take care not to break his neck picking the high Pippin trees. Indeed, William enjoyed an arrangement which few workmen shared in the 1850s. Eighty years after Enclosure, Henry Baldwyn was allowing William time off to work on his own smallholding, and now more time to pick the apples which William would buy off David Drinkwater and re-sell in Evesham market.

David Drinkwater's orchard was such a mixture of dessert apples, early and late, cooking apples, cider fruit, perry pears and some dessert pears. Grandfather and David knew which varieties to pick first, which to keep, and which to grind for cider or perry.

Four hundred varieties of apples grew in Great Britain in Grandfather's day, but to quote the Rev. John M. Wilson from his *Rural Cyclopaedia of Agriculture*, published in 1847, "Most of the varieties are deformed-looking objects and grievously offend the eye, yet very ornamental when in blossom." He was writing of the trees rather than the fruit, but is was also true how some unattractive looking varieties of apples yet had a fragrance, a kind of bouquet, all of their own.

The Early Margaret, fit to eat in July; the Seek No Farther in September; Summer Pearmains and Codlins; later, the Ribston Pippen, the Grey Runet, the Spice Apple, Tom Putts, that rosy red-yellow fleshed but unevenly shaped fruit, aptly branded as Nine Squares. For winter storing there was Nelson, Queen Charlotte, Shenn's Kernel, Crump's Kernel. For early baking, an apple which cooked to a froth, nothing ever excelled Ecklinville. Normantons and Manchester Pippins followed later. Lord Grosvenor would either cook or eat; Princess Pippins grew on grafted crab apple trees and were favoured by the autumn visiting velts or field-fares when they swarmed the hedgerows.

The varieties in Mr. Baldwyn's orchards were more numerous still. The Golden Harvery Bittersweets, good for mincemeat making, Keswick Codlings, Sourings. The Rev. Wilson's *Rural Cyclopaedia* says Loan's Pearmain is a beautiful middle-sized fruit, its colour red towards the sun, striping with red to the shade, and its flesh has a vinous flavour, but soon becomes mellow.

So every day that week William picked hampers and skips of the fine apples in David Drinkwater's orchard. Mary Ann took little Phoebe along and she slept on a bed of hay in a pot hamper, while her mother picked up the fruit which had fallen to the ground.

Taught by David Drinkwater, William always put a little straw in the bottom of each hamper and placed his fruit carefully to avoid bruising. From time immemorial, the merchants expected to find the finest apples on the top layer, so the toppers were picked and placed but never with the intention to deceive the shrewd market buyers who would empty fruit from hamper to hamper if they suspected bad packing, and who would themselves also place the best fruit in the front of their shops, keeping the less handsome behind.

Wednesdays and Thursdays were William's days for taking his apples in to Evesham market. It made a long day for him, starting for town as soon as daylight came, sitting in front of his little cart, while Ned the donkey took his time to walk the six miles. William was stuck at the roadside some mornings because Ned refused to pass a ragged tramp on his way to Tewkesbury workhouse.

"You need summat to rattle behind his hind legs, bwoy," Long Fred told him. "A piece of old iron on a string."

William found a worn-out breast plough share in the hedge at the back of his garden; one that Thomas had left behind, no doubt. He tied a length of string to the share and carried it with him on the cart so that when the donkey refused to move he dropped it into the road in front of the near side wheel and it made a clanking sound. Ned would put his long ears forward and break into a trot, though not for long. The plough share behind his tail worked much better than the proverbial carrot-under-the-nose method with Ned, who was never particularly hungry on the road. After all, weren't carrots and parsnips fed liberally into his manger at home. So to offer him a carrot was no better than giving him a strawberry.

In those pre-Christmas days when Grandfather's cart took the fruit to Evesham, the buyers couldn't always get Blenheim Orange, the favoured dessert apple of the day, but they knew there was a ready market for the tried and trusted varieties, like Court Pondu Plait, a French Blenheim, which was smaller than its relative, and Lady's Dessert ate well at Christmas also.

Grandfather dealt well and fairly with the Evesham merchants, having learnt a lot of the art and mystery of the trade from David Drinkwater. The Evesham buyers had a language of their own for criticising the villagers' fruit: as sour as varges, or verjuice; mella, for a mellow apple; roxy for the over-ripe; rivelled for an after-Christmas Blenheim, and so on.

At the end of the day Grandfather's chief worry was getting his empty hampers back from the buyers, hampers marked by Mary Ann with a W.A. in black paint on the brown withy. It was often nearly dark when Ned and William passed the Town Hall at Evesham on their way home over the Avon Bridge. Stop-go it would be all the way, for every time a bird rustled roosting in the roadside thicket Ned stopped, pointed his long ears forward and looked apprehensively into the hedge. The main road now had a reasonable surface, but it was a rough mile from the main road up the Groaten, then round by the village cross, for the wheel ruts made by the Squire's waggons were filled with stones, and the donkey cart jolted over these, tossing William with his empty hampers. Grandfather often said how good it was to see the light in their cottage window and to meet Mary Ann who held a horn lantern at the stable door as he unharnessed the donkey. Home to him, he said, was when the cottage door opened, and Phoebe met him with uncertain steps on the flagstones, and he could smell the boiled bacon and cabbage from the range, and another day was over.

David Drinkwater's apples were picked that week, but the cider fruit remained to be shaken from the trees of Black Tauntons. William did this with a long larch pole out of Ashton Wood with an iron hook at the end, and Mary Ann, Millie Watchet and Joe Salter picked them in baskets, then put them in sacks ready for the cider making. The best cider was made from the smaller fruit, too small for market, mixed with the traditional cider varieties like Fox Whelps and Black Tauntons. As with grapes, there were the vintage years when the hot summer sun ripened the fruit, which was stored in sacks at the tree butts until November, increasing the sugar content.

David Drinkwater made quite a number of hogshead barrels of cider. He had told William that if he helped to make it at the mill at Bumbo he could have a barrel for himself. Mary Ann had mixed feelings about that; she knew how her husband liked to entertain his friends at the cider barrel. A hogshead, she thought, was rather a lot, what with the barrels of parsnip wine, rhubarb wine and methogalum, made like mead from honey-comb. Mary was able to keep William moderate

118

in his habits and weekly on Sunday he heard the
Methodists warn the little flock of the dangers of drink.
But he liked his cider with his fat bacon and the bread
that Mary Ann baked every fortnight in the oven heated
by faggots of gorse off Bredon Hill.

Adding water to apple juice to make cider is as old as
the hills, but there are variations. The cheese husk, or
pomace, from the press, if steeped in water for twelve
hours will yield a good family drink, says one writer,
and a poem on cider by the seventeenth-century poet
John Philips confirms this.

> . . . Thou most wise, shall steep
> Thy husks in water, and again employ
> Thy ponderous engine (The Mill) . . .
> . . . Water will imbibe
> The small remains of spirit, and acquire
> A vinous flavour, this the peasant blithe
> Will quaff, and whistle, as the tinkling team
> They drive and sing of Fusca's radiant eyes,
> Pleased with the medley draught . . .

"Benevolent, I allus feels, when I drink a few pints of
Drink-water's cider," William would say. But perhaps
Philips had a point about making the less potent drink;
harvest cider it was called in Ashton. Some stuff called
Stunum was stronger, but did make some men
quarrelsome; not a good thing in the harvest field.

Importing apples and pears out of season from
sunnier lands was of course something the countryman
of Grandfather's day knew next to nothing about, so

119

the home-grown varieties were looked forward to in their turn, as much as the rising larks in February and the April cuckoo. Especially the pears, which came and went so much more quickly than the apples.

A lot of Drinkwater's pear trees were grafted on hawthorn and the shoots of May showed white, as the snow-covered pear blossom had a month earlier. The Jargonelle pear grew well against the cottage walls; sweet as honey, a summer benefit. Summer Boncretien, the Little Green Chisel and the larger Green Windsor were in supply in August. Autumn heralded the Great Mouth Water, a fruit where the juice ran in rivulets down the chin. Pitmaston Duchess, the pear which weighed nearly a pound, was sought after by the Evesham merchants. William Archer laid these gently down on a straw bed in Drinkwater's barn until, a month after, the green turned to yellow and pink on the skin, then they were hampered for market.

A fine pear from Worcester nurseries, not like the Black Pear of Worcester, so hard and sour until the spring, when even then, it was what's known as a choker, Louis-Bonne had flavour of its own. When ripe the juice was fragrant nectar but what an unattractive fruit, mis-shapen, scabby, yet under that uninviting peel the exquisite flavour lay.

Grandfather soon learned that pears were fickle fruit compared with apples. "Keep 'um another wick, a wick too soon and they be too far gone." Roxy, the Evesham men said.

Perry, the fermented juice of that swan egg, the Malvern Hill pear, or the little Hazel pear, was made in less quantity than cider at David Drinkwater's farm. "Can be a bit purging," old Fred Dunn warned. "Run for the hedge and be beaten to it by the last trouser button."

No fruit in David Drinkwater's orchard was ever wasted. Fallen Drunken Wills, bruised by the autumn gales, were too unripe for cider, so they went for pig feed. But William stood the sound ones on beds of straw in Mr. Drinkwater's barn and watched them turn a primrose yellow colour with an orange flush on the skin. Every Wednesday and Thursday he took his load to Evesham and, as Christmas drew near and the fruit trade grew brisker, he sometimes hired a waggon instead of the cart.

"Thee bring as many a them yella apples, and some Blenheims to the markit, next wick for my shop, 'ull ya, William?" urged Charlie Joiner, as he stood there in his cord trousers and sleeved waistcoat.

"Wednesday for sure, Charlie," William answered.

The Tuesday evening William loaded the donkey cart well above the side raves and roped on the hampers of apples, leaving just enough room at the front for him to sit on his bolting of straw. William usually took a bolting of straw to Evesham and sold it for sixpence to one of the market gardeners who worked on the black soil of the Abbey land. They grew patches of early radishes and forced them under wheat straw in January. William was proud of his load of fruit as he took his donkey and cart down Ashton village street next morning, where he met Spider on his way to work and

Alf Stubbs bringing in his team of horses nose to tail, haltered from the fields.

The load jolted over the rough wheel ruts, then, as he approached the village cross just opposite Stanley Farm, the nearside wheel of the cart slipped off the axle sending the apples from the hampers rolling in the gutter. I suppose he lost about a couple of pots of apples and he was lucky that Alf Stubbs came by with Spider.

They unloaded the cart and lifted the axle into a wheelbarrow from the farm, slid the wheel back in place and fetched a spare cotter pin from Jim Dance's stable, allowing William to continue his journey. That was the last time Grandfather William saw Alf Stubbs.

It happened in this way. Squire Baldwyn decided to drain the Big Thurness, that heavy land adjoining Umberlands Lane. For this he needed a supply of clay pipes from Dumbleton Brick and Tile Works, the concern owned by his neighbour, Squire Edward Holland. Four-inch pipes were two pounds five shillings per thousand and two-inch pipes were eighteen shillings and six pence per thousand. After he'd worked out what was needed, he sent Alf Stubbs, his carter, to fetch the load.

Alf Stubbs was used to the Dumbleton road and took two horses to haul the pipes from the kilns. It happened that Thursday morning, the day after he had helped William with the upset load of apples, that Alf put a young three-year-old cart horse in the shafts with an old mare, in long gears as trace horse. Coming down the hill towards Dewrest Lane, the filler in the shafts was obliged to stand well back in the breeching, so that the breeching against his hind quarters held back the load.

Young Sharper, the filler that day, was not used to holding back such a heavy load as the drain pipes. He pottered between the shafts and let the load overrun him. Alf held the rein on the mullen, or bridle, so that Sharper's bit was pulled well back in his mouth. He responded, and the load was in control. But down the steep part of Rabbit Lane, the breeching chain pulled the staple from the shaft with the weight of the load. The shafts shot forward with the force and weight of the loaded cart. The nearside shaft struck Alf at the back of his head fracturing his skull and the cart wheel passed over his body. Alf was found by an estate worker, killed in the Rabbit Lane.

Sad it was in a small village for such a tragedy to happen. Sad the villagers were when William, Fred Dunn, Jim Dance and Walter Peart wheeled Alf in his coffin on the bier down to St. Barbara's churchyard. Spider tolled the bell as they wound their way past the drooping ash trees to the church. The coffin was plain elm with a margin of black around the edges, like the black on the mourning cards. Everything was black, except the flowers, black gloves, black bowler hats, black jackets. Lotty Stubbs walked with Mary Ann and Martha Dunn. It appeared she had no relatives, but came to Ashton as a girl to work in service for Mrs. Baldwyn. Archdeacon Timbrell conducted the short service and at the graveside Spider wept as he sprinkled the fine soil on the coffin when the Vicar recited the familiar words.

So the group of cottagers was split now. Alf had left the company of William, Fred and Spider, and Fred hauled the pipes to the Big Thurness until the Squire found another carter to take the place of Alf Stubbs.

CHAPTER
FOURTEEN

A Breeches and Gaiters Job

"I see Squire Baldwyn's niece is sweethearting with a parson from Berkeley way," Spider remarked to William Archer in the little kitchen of the White Hart Inn which adjoined William's garden.

"Oi, young Reuben Dunn as drives the Earl's coach told me when he was up here, staying at Fred and Martha's, that this parson and the Earl don't see eye to eye in Tyndal village," William replied.

Alan Moncrieff was a man always very proud of his pure English descent — despite his Scottish surname. His grandmother, who eloped with William Moncrieff, was a very considerable heiress, but she reared seventeen children and the family fortune was divided. On leaving school he had worked for a time with his cousin's firm of solicitors before taking Holy Orders. His first curacy was at Rowley Regis in the heart of the Black Country, where he rejoiced to find he was able to use his physical strength to the full in his new service. "Hard as any toad," he was described by the admiring miners, and the Reverend was often called out to stop fights and riots. It was also remembered of him that he was visiting, nursing and burying through a ghastly smallpox epidemic, out without an overcoat in all weathers and at all hours of the day or night.

After being appointed temporary Rector of Tyndal the Rev. Alan Moncrieff often came up from the Berkeley Vale to see Miss Augusta Baldwyn. He preached at St. Barbara's church by invitation of Archdeacon Timbrell and became quite a figure in Ashton, noticed as a man who marched rather than walked down the village street, carrying his overcoat from the end of a blackthorn stick over his shoulder, his sleeves rolled up and wearing the heaviest of nailed boots. Short and sturdy of build, almost as broad as he was tall, and immensely strong physically, he was a mighty walker; a fearer of God and of nothing else; without any sense of caste. He was also a lover of all things connected with the country, fiercely independent and impatient of authority. He was a tramp by nature with a love for all other wanderers, ready to use his fists with all and sundry. He was of the true Borrow breed. A Conservative by tradition, yet he was far too independent a thinker to be a member of any political party. He had Cobbett's intense hatred of any kind of tyranny. This was the man the Earl of Tyrconnel had as his neighbour and Rector at Tyndal in Berkeley Vale.

Now the Earl had two nephews, the elder, young Sean, was studying to take Holy Orders at Oxford. He was only in his first year but already the Earl had it in mind for him to become Vicar of Tyndal, since the living was in the Earl's gift as Lord of the Manor. So

126

Alan Moncrieff entered an agreement with the Earl to hold the living at Tyndal parish until Sean had taken Holy Orders, when he would vacate in his favour.

One of his parishioners the temporary Rector visited most zealously meanwhile was Sam Tombs, who had been the Earl's bailiff since he left the Manor at Beckford and Squire Wakeman. Sam had been ill for some months after an attack of rheumatic fever and Alan Moncrieff used to bring him presents of fruit from the Rectory. When Sam eventually died, the Rector asked Mrs. Tombs who she would like to carry her husband's body to the grave in the little churchyard at Tyndal.

"Oh, his friends from Ashton, if that's possible. William Archer, Spider Watchet, Fred Dunn and Walter Peart," she replied.

The Rector talked with the Earl about this, who agreed to send his coachman to Ashton to bring the men down for the funeral. William remembered that February afternoon when the icy wind was sweeping across the churchyard, standing there beside the Rector with the other bearers from Ashton. Alan Moncrieff was reading the familiar words at the graveside, "For as much as it hath pleased Almighty God of His great mercy to take unto Himself the soul of our dear brother here departed", when he paused and looked at the shivering mourners. He remarked quietly, inclining his head towards the coffin, "I'm sure our dear brother here departed wouldn't mind if we all put our hats on."

"We did," William said, "and Sam never objected."

So Sam Tombs died and the Earl was without a bailiff.

The day after the funeral Spider, Fred Dunn and Walter Peart returned to Ashton in the coach driven by Reuben Dunn, Fred's son, and Reuben was allowed to stay with his parents overnight at Ashton. William stayed on at Tyndal with George and Ada Bass.

"'A would like a word with you, Archer, about entering my employment," the Earl said to him after the funeral. "Stay a few days and think over the prospect of becoming my bailiff."

"I don't know about staying here, sir, because I'm supposed to be draining at Squire Baldwyn's," replied William.

But the Earl assured the young man that all had been taken care of. He and the Squire understood each other and a letter had gone by Reuben Dunn to the Earl's old friend Henry Baldwyn.

William stayed over the weekend and was amazed at the congregation in church that Sunday. "The whole village turned out and crowded the church with the choir and church band," he told my Uncle Fred. The Funeral Anthem was performed with all possible pomp and ceremony, the words taken from Alexander Pope's ode, "The dying Christian to his soul":

> Vital spark of heav'nly flame!
> Quit, O quit this mortal frame:
>   Trembling, hoping, ling'ring, flying,
>   Oh the pain, the bliss of dying!

Cease, fond Nature, cease thy strife,
And let me languish into life.

After church on Sunday, the Rev. Moncrieff invited
William to his house. A bachelor Rectory it was, cold
and bare. An old housekeeper who had cooked and
cleaned there for fifty years got them some supper.

"You're coming to be bailiff for the Earl then,
William, ay," said the Rector.

"'Tis a good offer, sir, indeed," William replied. "But
I don't know whether I can follow Sam Tombs," he
added.

"Going back in the morning, are you?"

"Yes, I'm gwain be train to Bredon station on the
new Gloucester line. Never bin be train afore, sir,"
William said with a certain amount of apprehension.

"Oh, you'll be all right, young fella, though going
through the tunnel near Charfield may give you a bit of
a surprise. But when you get to Ashton just take this
message to Miss Baldwyn, will you." And Alan
Moncrieff handed Grandfather an envelope.

Over supper William told the Rector how much he
had been touched by the regard of the village folk for
Sam who had been his friend in Ashton since they were
boys. "Oh, I've conducted several funerals since I came
here to Tyndal," Alan Moncrieff said. "Now it is sad
when someone like Sam dies, a relatively young man,
but a funeral here a month or so back was different.
The woman was a hundred and two." The Rector went
on to tell William about her funeral. It was the custom
in those days to tack in tinsel on the coffin lid the

initials and age of the deceased. The coffin maker in Tyndal couldn't read or write very well, and Alan Moncrieff was amazed to see that the old lady's age had become one thousand and two on her coffin.

"You've made her a thousand and two, you old fool," the Rector told the coffin maker at the graveside.

"I know I ahn't. One and two nowts maake a hundred, dooan't they? And a two maakes a hundred an' two!" he replied hotly.

William laughed. "I'm no scholar, sir, but I can see your meaning. But does your dog always sit by the grave like he did on Friday?"

"Oh yes, and when he hears the passing bell at another church he does the same. People accept it in a kind way, William, you know."

On the train next morning with the note for Miss Baldwyn, Grandfather thought deeply about the chance of becoming the Earl's bailiff. At home Mary Ann and young Phoebe met him as he walked down Bredon Hill to the cottage. It was night time before he told Mary Ann of the offer at Tyndale. As he wound up the grandfather clock at nine o'clock and went to bed, Mary Ann suggested that they thought it over for a week. But she wondered what would happen to the holding at Carrants Field and the donkey.

No one said much at the time, but everyone knew that George Archer was courting Lotty Stubbs, Alf's widow. Alf who had been killed by the cart in Rabbit Lane. "I suppose you'll go and live with Lotty when you're wed, George," William said as they met at the pump, drawing water in the early morning before work.

"No, she wants to get away from the place and thoughts of Alf," George replied. "Her still frets for him summat cruel, dost know."

"How about living at my place and working Carrants Field for a couple of years," William said to his brother.

"Where bist thee gwain to then. Not to Caneder happen?" George dropped his bucket of water and pushed back his billycock hat so stunned he was by William's suggestion.

"Berkeley Vale," William said. "Bailiff to the Earl of Tyrconnel."

"Damn it, that's a breeches and gaiters job, un't it, a bailiff, but I'll see ya when I've seen Lotty. Bailiff ay, William Archer, bailiff." George carried his two buckets of water on the yokes to his cottage.

On his way to the meet at Elmley Castle that week Squire Henry Baldwyn passed a field known as Pecked Meadow where Spider and William were draining the pasture land, channelling their two-inch pipes into a four-inch master drain which emptied into Carrants Brook near the turnpike. "Lord Tyrconnel fancies you as his new bailiff, then, William," he said.

"Yes, master, and Mary Ann and I have decided to go to Tyndal if you can release me from the draining and the harvesting," William replied nervously.

"I've told the Earl that you can be spared for a couple of years if your brother George will take your place working with Spider," Henry Baldwyn stated.

So it was agreed and George Archer cultivated Carrants Field, while William and Mary Ann packed their few things ready for the move to Tyndal. William looked hard at the grandfather clock as he wound it up that last evening at nine, and the tears came to Mary Ann's eyes as she watched her husband pull the chains and the great lead weights rise in the case.

"Seems a pity to move it, Will," she said.

William regarded the clock face and the pink flowers around the hours, he listened to the chime as it struck nine o'clock, then said softly, "We'll leave it yere in the front room. George 'ull look after it for ma."

The journey to Tyndal was Mary Ann's first ride on the train. Spider and Millie Watchet walked over Bredon Hill to Bredon station to see them off and their young Henry came to say goodbye to his friend, Phoebe.

The house on the Earl's estate where Sam Tombs had lived as bailiff was not vacant until Lady Day, when Sam's widow was moving into a cottage in Tyndal village. So William and Mary and Phoebe went to stay with George and Ada Bass, who were tenants on the estate, until that date. George and Ada made them very welcome, but William noticed how the couple had both aged since they left Beckford and, despite their frequent visits to Bath and the waters of that spa, they were crippled with rheumatism. George Bass was a good friend to Grandfather. It was he who gave him the secret of growing teasels, an alien plant to William, but one which grew by the acre on the damp lush land near the Severn, and was supplied to the cloth mills of Stroud. George also gave his young friend some advice.

"Come along with me to church Sunday, William. I know your Methody leaning, but 'twill look better.

Great believer I be in holding the candle to our Rector. His word goes a long way in the Parish."

William Archer took due notice of these words of George Bass and he was at Evensong in Tyndal church on Sunday. William, despite his inability to read or write, very much loved to sing and he loved the Rev. Moncrieff's choice of hymns, the verses of such writers as Watts and Addison, sung to the old rolling eighteenth-century tunes. Alan Moncrieff loathed what he called the frothy pap poured every Sunday into the ears of worldly folk. There was nothing anaemic about the Christ he worshipped.

The Earl of Tyrconnel sat with the younger members of his family in the Squire's pew, which reminded William of the Baldwyn pew at St. Barbara's church at Ashton.

William discovered that the estate finances were managed by an agent and that the Earl required him to supervise the cultivation of the strong arable land, the planting and harvesting of the crops and the care of the cattle and sheep. The Tyndal estate, the ancestral home of the Tyrconnels, skirted the River Severn to the north and the Cotswold edge to the south; it was Vale land, flooded in the lower fields by the river and the Severn bore, that high tide which sweeps up stream from the Bristol Channel. Even in early spring William found the grass was green on the river banks and the ruby red Hereford cattle with their white faces contrasted in the spring sunshine with the purple muddy river, the greens of the Forest of Dean on the other side of the river, and the mellow Cotswold stone walls and houses to the south.

William had been the Earl of Tyrconnel's bailiff but three months when news came that the Earl's eldest nephew, Sean, was dead. "My nephew has died at Oxford," the Earl said abruptly to the Rector.

"So I hear," Alan Moncrieff replied.

"Now my other nephew is starting at university and I shall expect him to take the living here when he has finished his studies."

Alan Moncrieff listened to the Earl with apparent disinterest, but replied quite calmly, "I entered into an agreement with you that I would vacate the living at Tyndal in favour of your nephew, Sean. Now Sean has died and I shall stay, for no other agreement has been made in favour of any other member of your family."

The Earl was furious and made all manner of threats to no avail. For Alan Moncrieff was not a humble man, no milk and water parson, but a determined cleric, reminiscent of the old-time Squarson.

Perhaps more than the rest of the village, Grandfather had a grandstand view of all the stages in the quarrel between the Squire and Alan Moncrieff, but he and George Bass, as bailiff and tenant to Lord Tyrconnel, were obliged to hold their peace on the subject.

Although William Archer and his little family were living in the rich Vale of the Severn, they found poverty amongst the labourers on the land as pinching as in the Vale of Evesham. The Earl administered the Meat Charity, a legacy left by his ancestors. Three bullocks were killed with three fat sheep, producing nineteen hundredweights of meat. There was great difficulty in the distribution owing to the crowd of people. The local paper reported that Meat Tickets should have been given to the deserving poor, but that instead the strongest fared best, whilst others went empty-handed.

On the Rectory land was a duck pond where Alan Moncrieff kept a flock of Khaki Campbell ducks, the ancestors in fact of ducks kept at Ashton where they swam up and down the open stream in the village street fifty years after, when his son lived there. The Earl enclosed the Tyndal pond and filled it in, while his men planted a garden on the Rectory land. The Rev. Moncrieff made no objection, but he noted the actions of the Earl who controlled the living at Tyndal. Next the Earl ordered the dividing wall between his house and the Rectory to be knocked down and rebuilt closer to the Rector's house. Still the Rector took no action. Perhaps his theory was to carry a stone in his pocket a long time before he eventually threw it. He did however lock a door which divided the two properties and where the Earl's cows came twice daily through for the milking. In hot temper the Earl smashed down the door and drove his cows through the Rectory gardens doing some damage.

This was the last straw as far as Moncrieff was concerned; he took the Earl to court and claimed damages. Moncrieff won the day. The Squire was ordered to pay damages and restore the duck pond. This upset the Earl, who sold all rights to the living, refusing to have any more to do with the church until the Rev. Alan Moncrieff was replaced. This was not the first time Squire and Rector had been at odds in the Vale of Berkeley. George Bass told William of a similar feud in the previous century, when one parson had insisted on collecting his tithes in kind, claiming all the milk from the squire's cows every tenth day. The squire and the neighbouring farmers considered that he was only entitled to one milking every tenth day. So the dispute went to court. The farmers complained that the parson didn't collect the milk and that they could not spare the buckets. The parson said the farmers blocked the road and added a mile to the journey and that they put rennet in the milk to turn it sour. They also told the milkmaids not to rise early or strip out the cows on what they termed the devil's day, the day when the tithe was due, and again, the parson won the law suit.

One relief to the poverty of the times was when the Tyndal folk were given a day's outing to Clevedon that first summer William was bailiff for the Earl. The Earl chartered a pleasure boat at Oldbury on Severn which took the villagers via Beachley and Portishead to the seaside at Clevedon. On the return journey the company were entertained by Tochington Military Band. This fine band was still called military despite the fact that the regiment was disbanded in 1810. The report says that dancing (etc.) were freely indulged in. One wonders what was meant by (etc.). The day ended with a dance on the Green Wharf at Oldbury on Severn.

Always ready to see the funny side of life, whether it was at Ashton or Tyndale, William recounts a harvest scene, that first harvest in Berkeley Vale. A former bailiff in the Vale was surprised one day to come across one of the labourers pitching hay with his trousers off. "Harry, where are your trousers, you can't work in front of houses without your trousers," he called to the workman.

"Well, zur," Harry said, "we tapped a fresh barrel o' zider s'morning an thee knows't what fresh zider do do. Main purgin'. It've bin servin' I out crool, an' I've took me trousers down so often I thought 'twould save time like, if I lef' em off altogether. Just until the zider have done a working me."

William's first summer at Tyndale ended with the Harvest Festival at the church. There seemed to be an uneasy truce at this time of the year between the Earl and his Rector. William was ordered to convey several pot hampers of the finest apples, plums and pears to the Festival. Sheaves of wheat, sacks of potatoes and other produce of the farm and garden were also sent along by the Earl. He even attended Evensong but sat in a seat towards the rear of the nave and never again occupied the Squire's pew. Perhaps the two gentlemen thought in their heart of hearts that after all they had both acted in a childish manner.

The Harvest Festival at Tyndal inevitably turned William and Mary Ann to thinking of how Ashton folk had fared, how George had managed his harvest in Carrant Field, whether Spider was busy that autumn killing the cottagers' pigs and how Archdeacon Timbrell ruled at the church. Mary Ann especially longed for the company of the Watchets, the Pearts, the

Dunns and George's new wife, Lotty, who had been Lotty Stubbs. For George Archer had married quietly one Saturday at St. Barbara's church, before moving into William's cottage. So she was overjoyed when the Earl agreed to give William time off to go home and spend a weekend in Ashton.

The train from Gloucester drew into Bredon station and rather than climb the nine hundred and sixty feet of Bredon Hill, William decided to walk to Ashton through the Hill villages of Overbury and Conderton and Beckford. Along the Beckford road they met Squire Henry Baldwyn. "How are you getting on down at the Earl's estate?" the aged Squire enquired. "Now if you would like to come back here there is work for you, young fella."

"I'll stay a while, master, but Mary Ann misses the Ashton folk," William replied.

That weekend the Archers from Tyndal were entertained by George and Lotty. On Saturday afternoon William walked down Gypsies Lane with George to Carrants Field and was pleased to see the stubble ploughed, the potatoes in bury, the sprouts fit to pick and the parsnips ready to dig.

"I suppose Master Baldwyn does give you a day a so off to work Carrants Field, George?" William asked.

George was taken aback by this remark and replied, "Now don't it look as if somebody does some work down year."

"Tidy it is, George boy, and the donkey looks well, and the pig, I'd say, will be fit for Spider to butcher by Christmas. I'm satisfied, and to stand here looking at the brook coming under the bridge in the land and hearing the wood pigeons in the ivy up in the withy trees does make me feel loath to go back."

George stood by his brother and said quietly, "Come back yere to Ashton, 'cos it sounds to me by what you say about the trouble with the Rector and the Squire that 'tis not all honey down at Tyndal."

William answered after a while and told his brother that Mr. Baldwyn had offered him a job but he would have to stay another year with the Earl to be fair.

Saturday night at the White Hart Inn George and William sat with Spider, Long Fred, and young Joe Salter, Tilda's boy, and talked of the goings on in the village. Fred Dunn came in and the landlord drew him a quart of cider in his special mug. Fred always reckoned that a pint was no good for a start and had his quart. Then Walter Peart arrived with his Old English sheep dog, Rosie; he'd been looking round his ewes on Holcombe Nap.

Hanging his frail basket at the back of the door and putting his shepherd's crook in the corner by the fire he said, "Now, William, I suppose the yows all has double lambs down Berkeley way and they be all taps."

William was ready for a bit of banter from the village and replied, "No, but they sell sheep by the yard at Thornbury market."

"Don't thee talk so stupid, bwoy, none of my yows be above a yard long," the shepherd said as the others laughed.

"By the churchyard. Now un't that a yard, you chaps," William replied.

"That 'ull do," Spider said. "I'll put my hat on that tale."

As George and William walked home from the inn and said good night to their friends, Spider looked over the pigsty wall at the cottage and said to William, "George has got a pig in the sty, not like you, who kept a bear in there."

At the Methodist meeting on the Sunday William again renewed acquaintances, but when evening came his close friends sat around the fireside sampling the cider while Spider came along with a couple of the members of the Church Orchestra and played with the viols.

"Tell us about some of the folk at Tyndal, Mr. Archer," young Joe Salter, Tilda's boy, said. "I've heard about the Severn Bore."

"Have you heard the one about the Devil trying to move the Cotswold Hills?" William said.

"No," Joe replied. "Tell us, Mr. Archer."

"One of George Bass's tales this is." Then William told how the legend runs that the Devil got a great wheelbarrow and was wheeling the Cotswolds towards the Severn. He said that he would fill the Severn with the hills. Near Tyndal he was tired and met a cobbler who was mending his shoes, the soles of which were worn down to the uppers. 'How far is the Severn, cobbler,' the Devil asked. 'Oh, a long way, for I've worn out a pair of shoes walking from that river,' was the reply. So the Devil called it a day and tipped up the wheelbarrow and that's why there is a big hill at Tyndal."

"You shouldn't fill the boy's head with such rubbish," Mary Ann remonstrated, "and you as have been to the Methodists this morning to worship God. I don't know."

"Do you attend the Reverend Moncreiff's church at Tyndal?" Spider enquired.

"Oi, I goes along of George Bass and sits next to a fella they call the shrewd man. He's a man as taks a tidy bit of weighing up. Supposed to be a man with powers to heal. He goes about among the sick a saying the words, 'I have come to soothe your sorrow, heal your wounds and drive away your fear.' Ay, he took his hoss to the Sunday School treat in the summer and got the children to try and pull him backuds on a rope from the trace. Harmless they do say, but he plays his fiddle to the cows and says he gets more milk."

"To hear William talk tonight you would think there was no work done at Tyndal, but I'm telling you when he come home to bed he needs no rocking to go to sleep," Mary Ann said somewhat annoyed.

Spider wanted to know all about the church band at Tyndal, and whether it was as good as the one at Ashton in its heyday. Grandfather often told Dad what a loss to village church music it was when the Ashton band was eventually replaced by the dismal groans of a harmonium. It happened gradually, as old men left, as Sam Tombs had left. Lack of encouragement on the part of "progressive" parsons could be blamed for others not taking up the instruments played by their elders. The key bugles, sweetest of instruments, were the first to go. The clarinets lingered a while and then were heard no more. The tenor trombone was missing one morning, and his bass brother felt his loneliness so much that he gave up the struggle. At last the old bass viol was left all by itself. It's sad when I recall Dad's words. "It was so much honoured, and so ancient; yet one Sunday night it was placed in the faded green baize bag that had been its shelter, by the good old man who had played it from his youth, to be brought back no more. The harmonium had the field to itself."

After that weekend in Ashton it took a while for Grandfather and Mary Ann and young Phoebe to settle down again to life in Tyndal with its quarrels between Squire and Rector. Indeed, it was partly because of this continuing feud between his master, the Earl, and Alan Moncrieff that William decided he would leave Lord Tyrconnel's employment the following Michaelmas, after a stay of a little short of two years.

"I've heard from Henry Baldwyn and gather you would like to return, and I shall not stand in your way, William," said the Earl when my Grandfather asked his leave to come back to Ashton. The stay by the Severn side had been an experience for the Archer family.

As for Alan Moncrieff, his frequent visits to Ashton bore fruit. He married the Squire's niece, Augusta Baldwyn and, to the Earl's chagrin, stayed on at Tyndal until his death.

CHAPTER
FIFTEEN

A Tithe in Time

Squire Henry Baldwyn had been ailing for some time and the running of the estate had more and more been on the shoulders of his son William. When Henry died William honoured the promise his father had made to William Archer to find employment for him at Ashton. William was pleased to return to his native village but not more pleased than his wife Mary Ann, who had longed for her friends Millie, Martha and Lotty. Back in the village, Squire Baldwyn found a cottage for George Archer, to enable William to go back to his house near the White Hart Inn.

William was put in charge of the young Squire's new project on Bredon Hill, planting the larch plantation near Great Hill Barn. The Squire took a pride in the timber on the Manor farms and was anxious to grow larch on the Hill for fencing the fields in the Vale. The Hill fields were different. They were enclosed by stone walls, similar to the walls on nearby Cotswold hills.

"Good fences make good neighbours, William," he told Grandfather as his men were preparing timber at the saw pit near the Manor's bull pen.

William, Mary Ann and young Phoebe were soon busy in the time they had to spare, working in Carrants Field on the holding. George Archer, who had cultivated it while they were away at Tyndal, went into a partnership with his brother so that he and Lotty were able to share in the work and also share in the produce of the land.

"Do ya go along to Hill Cottage to Methodists Meetings now a day, George?" William asked his brother one day.

"Ah, 'tis a active service up there now we've bin taken over by Evesham and we hold Love Feasts every month."

George and Lotty explained how there was now a system of quarterly tickets in Ashton which were examined by the steward at each attendance. The tickets were dated and distinguished by a text about fleeing the wrath to come.

"All very particular," Lotty explained to Mary Ann. "If you slip up, your ticket is not renewed. If you are absent 'S' in the register means 'sick'; 'D' for 'distant' means you are away; 'B' is for 'on business'; and 'N' means 'neglect'."

"That's considered a sin," George said, "'neglect', and three times absent without a reason means you are out of the society."

The vigour of the little society at Ashton, however, was maintained steadily in those cottage meetings of the early 1860s. Archdeacon Timbrell viewed Ashton's fourteen members with suspicion, but as Squire Baldwyn said, "They are a harmless little section of the village, interfering with no one, and are among some of my best workers."

On a fine spring morning William left the house next to the White Hart early. All the men that could be spared were working near Great Hill Barn. The giant beech trees had not yet shown any signs of leaves. They stood black and cold in early spring, in a scene where only the elderberry bushes were green.

Fred Dunn, Long Fred and Neal were planting the young larch trees on the thin land where the stone outcrops of the parish quarry caught the morning sun, and William sang as he walked through the hamlet of Paris. He stopped and drank of the clear spring water which oozed from the hill above, running as it had from time immemorial down to feed the moat pond below. The pond used to be fished by the monks, and William, who had often picked up the odd piece of pottery here, had been told by Squire Baldwyn that here the Romans camped, sheltered by the woods on the Hill, and they had drunk at this very spring. William sang:

> For waters from the rock, once riven,
> By mercy's wondrous rod,
> For feasts of love, and tastes of heaven,
> All glory be to God.

That mid-summer Mary Ann gave birth to a son, my Uncle Jim, in the long bedroom at the back of their house near the White Hart. Little Phoebe was four years old now and pottering around the garden, feeding the pig, playing with the donkey, and soon would be

145

having lessons in the vestry of St. Barbara's church, for it was here that the children attended school.

After being our Vicar for sixty-eight years, Archdeacon Timbrell died at Beckford, aged ninety-six, and the Rev. Joseph Harrison and his wife took up residence at the Vicarage. He and the young curate took it in turns to teach the children simple reading and arithmetic, with an emphasis on the Catechism and the Prayer Book. Folk missed the Archdeacon, for with his jet black horses and Fred Dunn's son Reuben as his coachman in a cockaded hat he had cut an impressive figure in the countryside. Workers in the field would touch their hats when he rode by and women curtsied. Joseph Harrison was a very different character. Still somewhat of the John Bull breed, broad shouldered and having the appearance of a farmer, he was more one of the people than his predecessor, a visitor of the poor, a friend of the children. I suppose it could be said that he, like Naaman in the Bible, had one failing. Not leprosy, of course, but he was very fond of a social glass — too fond in fact. But like many who have that disability, he was generous to the extreme.

Carrant Field belonged to the Church and the rent from those acres were a part of the Vicar's stipend. William Archer paid his rent at Michaelmas and at Lady Day. Always prompt on time he had been when he paid Archdeacon Timbrell. The coins kept in the stocking were carefully held by Mary Ann.

"When do I get your rent, William?" the new Vicar asked Grandfather, as he accompanied the bell ringers singing their Christmas carols that year at Beckford

Vicarage. William made a habit of helping the bell ringers with the singing.

"Oh, March 25th, Lady Day. I allus paid Master Timbrell on that quarter day."

"I see," the Vicar replied, "another three months." As the ringers departed, he stopped Grandfather. "I'd like a word with you, William, before you go. Come into the kitchen and sit yourself down."

"Nothing wrong I hope, sir," William ventured haltingly.

"Drink that cup of cider and eat that piece of pie and tell me how the crops have been down by Carrants Brook."

William had never had a conversation like this with a parson before. The truth was he had only known two parsons, the Rev. Timbrell and the Rev. Moncrieff.

"Four sovereigns the rent is and you say it's due Lady Day. Now if you pay me three sovereigns this week, we will say the matter is settled until Michaelmas. That's if you have got three sovereigns by you, of course, William."

Grandfather was taken back a bit and answered, "Mary Ann sees to the money and holds the rent book. I'll have to ask her because I can neither read nor write."

"Come down here New Year's Day. Bring the money, and your wife, and the book will be receipted," he replied.

So New Year's Eve Mary Ann reached the rent book off the top of the grandfather clock, putting it in her bag with three sovereigns, and on New Year's Day,

147

William, his wife, Phoebe and baby Jim, drove along Grafton Road down Rabbit Lane to Beckford Vicarage with the donkey and cart. Joseph Harrison and his wife made them welcome in the kitchen. William drank cider and ate cake with his landlord while Mary Ann sipped her tea in front of the kitchen fire with Mrs. Harrison.

"Tell no one what has happened tonight," the Vicar said to William. "This is private business between us."

William nodded, but he wondered when the next rent would be called for. He need not have wondered because this little scene was enacted over and over again as long as he rented Carrants Field. Twenty-five per cent discount if he paid in advance. So the understanding between William and the new Vicar was established.

The Rev. Harrison often walked down Gypsies Lane over the brook bridge to the holding at Carrants Field. At dinner time he'd sit awhile in William's hovel on a pig bench by the stove, among the small tools of a market gardener. When the weather was wet the Vicar knew that William would be in his hovel sheltering from the rain. He might be shelling a few broad beans he had saved for seed, or placing his early potato seed in trays, or fixing a new stale or stick into a fork.

William's rhubarb or parsnip wine was relished by the Vicar on these visits. It made the sun shine in the souls of both the men. "I'll be planting the sprouts tomorrow if the rain baits," William said one afternoon around the stove. The Vicar nodded looking through the window at the drenched ground and the patch of sprout plants outside the hovel door.

"Ah," William continued, "you know what they allus told me when I was a bwoy. 'Don't keep it off the ground', the rain they meant, and some said 'It's a few too many spots on one', but a wet day does give me the time to do odd jobs in the hovel."

William continued to attend the Methodist meetings on Sunday mornings, but because he respected the Rev. Harrison and did not wish to give him offence, he started going to Evensong at St. Barbara's in Ashton.

"A good man, the Rev. Harrison is," William told the Squire as he was working with the men amongst the larch plantation on Bredon Hill.

"Ah, maybe," Mr. Baldwyn replied, "but don't you encourage his drinking your wine in Carrants Field hovel."

"No harm in we two on wet days. You see, sir, 'tis only one day among many and not like some folk who when the weather is unkind have what's known as a session, or a week on the drink."

"Don't do as I do, but do as I tell you," was what the Rev. Harrison said so often from the pulpit. There were times when the school children came home early because their teacher was inclined to fall asleep during lessons. And sometimes, it was true, he did get mixed up at a wedding when he started quoting from the funeral service. But Grandfather told Dad that Joseph Harrison's excesses were far outweighed by the charity he did in the parish. And I'm sure our village felt much more secure with the Rev. Harrison caring for the spiritual wellbeing of the parish than it did with the coach-riding magistrate, Archdeacon Timbrell.

Joseph Harrison was not an autocrat. He felt for the poor and their suffering and was surely a man for his time.

CHAPTER
SIXTEEN

Fred Dunn's Horses

On an acreage of farm land such as Squire Baldwyn's there were several four-horse teams, but Fred Dunn, head carter, was allowed the pick of the bunch when he went to plough. Fred Dunn's life revolved around what he called the team. Indeed, Charles Lamb could have had Fred for a model when he wrote about a carter and his horses, and how the man's dinner would be getting sadly dry in the oven until he had fed his horses, those strong, meek-eyed, submissive beasts.

Most of the heavy shire horses that were kept in Boss Close and Ten Furlongs were fit to do a good day's work. Sound in wind and limb, good workers in all gears, were the terms which could be applied to the Squire's beasts. Fred's favourite team for ploughing the autumn stubbles were Turpin as foremost, seventeen and a half hands, a five-year-old gelding; and Blossom, seventeen hands, a seven-year-old mare as second in the team, the lash horse. She was the mother of three-year-old Jolly, another gelding who acted as body horse; with Captain, a six-year-old gelding, as filler.

The filler was hooked directly into the plough and, apart from the trace harness, or long gears, carried a cart saddle to hold the ridge chain which kept the traces up. The other three horses in line had their traces hooked into the harness of the horse following.

Captain was what Fred Dunn termed "old in the yud", artful on the headland, apt to run askew instead of pulling the plough straight out to the end of the furrow. Fred had a leading rein on this filler horse and when the plough would stay in the clayland, he loosed the plough tails or handles and led Captain on the headland, helping the boy. "Cyaptin," Fred would call. "Cup now think I stole ya." The filler shook his head, the boy cracked his whip and the team pulled together as one.

Fred Dunn's favourite in the team was Blossom, the lash horse. Now seven years old, she had been bought by Squire Baldwyn as a yearling filly at Gloucester market. She was liver chestnut in colour, rather lighter legged than Turpin, with less feather around her fetlocks. Blossom was never intended to be a brood mare. The Squire had bred enough foals from some of the older mares on the Hill. But one Sunday in May, when Fred's horses were having their Sabbath rest in Boss Close, he walked, as was his custom, through the gardens of the hamlet of Paris and noticed that the young mare was missing. The gate into Clay Furlong was partly open, open enough to show the hoof marks of a cart horse in the soft clay. Fred followed the path towards Grafton thinking as he walked that no doubt Blossom was "in use" and looking for a mate. As the old saying goes, it's the willing horse as gets put on, so to speak, and his suspicions were right, of course, for

152

the mare was in a neighbour's field with some more mares turned out with a great roan coloured stallion. Fred slipped a halter on Blossom and brought her back to his horse field, but it was too late. Blossom had "stole the horse". It happens. So when she foaled and Jolly was born eleven months after, Fred called him his love child.

At three years old Jolly was still growing. His colour followed the stallion, a reddish roan. Fred broke him in the team for a while as a two year old, then turned him on the Hill to grow. "Never overwork a green horse," Fred said, "'Tis apt to stunt 'um."

I remember Grandfather saying the same thing. It takes about three or four years to get a horse handy for work, then he has got another twenty in front of him, if he has a good home. A two year old fresh to the collar will sweat and with a few days' work, and Sunday rest, will be "collar proud" on a Monday morning; not very inclined for work, snatching and jibbing in the traces. But Jolly was past that now, and an honest, reliable member of the four-horse team.

Turpin, foremost horse, was a good example of those ancestors of the shire horse, the black horses of the Midlands. He was out of a mare now retired to the Hill, by a travelling stallion from Winchcombe. Fred, like his fellow workers, spoke with a certain spleen of Winchcombe, down in its hollow. "Looks black over Winchcombe hole, you," he'd say when there was rain about, and Winchcombe was also labelled "Over Bill's Mother's." But Turpin was a good horse from the Winchcombe stallion. His mole-thick coat shone like

153

silk. Apart from a white star on his forehead and the white feather covering his fetlocks over his black hooves, Turpin was all black.

As the team walked slowly up and down those furrows along Beckfords Way, Turpin had a habit of snorting in the frosty seven o'clock morning air, sending whiffs of steam from his great nostrils. Then, as the day advanced, the steam from the sweat of his shoulders hung as a little cloud above his neck while the white foam-like lather weeped like cream from the crupper under his tail.

As foremost in the team, Turpin gave a real impression of great strength. His wide shoulders pressed against his collar, the way he carried his head bridled by the blinkered mullen with the polished horse brass over the white star on his forehead daunted the twelve-year-old plough boy who worked with Fred Dunn. As the team approached the headland at the end of each furrow, Turpin knew that he had to use every bit of his great power, tightening his traces until he brushed the hawthorn hedge with his nose. The boy cracked his whip as he walked the unploughed stubble. This made Turpin make a grunting noise as if to say, "I know, boy, I'm pulling my weight."

The boy grasped the rein with his left hand and turned, walking backwards to the left, what Fred Dunn called turning "come agun" or "come again". Holding the whip in his left hand the boy made each horse in turn pull the plough to the hedge, leaving Captain, the filler, to pull it alone the last few yards as the three in front had turned. At the other end of the field, the team

154

turned to the right, or turned "junkum", if the ploughman was casting a bed of ploughland.

Obviously, there were going to be a few horses which never fitted the bill. Left-handed ones, Fred Dunn called them, knock-kneed, ridge-backed, and the old stagers pensioned off on Bredon Hill, more than thirty years old. Then there was a durgin, an undersized cart horse, named Blackbird. Blackbird just didn't fit into any team. Because he was small, the other trace horses would always pull down on the collar on his shoulders, unless he was put as foremost horse. And that was out of the question, for the biggest animal had to have that place in front of the four in line. Blackbird had another disability. He only had one eye. The grown-up folk in the village never knew how he lost the sight of an eye, but the boys knew which one it was who carelessly threw the stone that partly blinded Blackbird one Sunday afternoon.

Fred Dunn had a soft spot for the little durgin, and used him for carting the hay from the rickyard to the tallet above the stable. Because he never went to town or was seen in the village street, Blackbird wore some of the poorest harness around for his short journeys. But Fred kept a handful of bean flour in the big pocket of his corduroy jacket and whenever he met Blackbird in the yard or the field, the little black horse would come up to Fred and nuzzle his pink nose into that pocket until Fred gave him a handful of ground beans.

To say Blackbird was a character would be true, the understanding between him and Fred was hard to explain. The rattle of the corn bin lid in the stable always made every one of the eight horses in the main stable turn round and strain on the leather straps which held them, like big dog collars, to the manger. Blackbird was never tied up in this fashion, but stood in a corner by the manger under the hay rack above. When Fred opened the corn bin to feed his charges with the ground oats and beans, Blackbird would saunter towards him and stand in front of the carter with his one eye, rivelling up his nose to show his front teeth, as much as to say, "Me first with the bait, Fred".

One wonders if the horses who had been at the plough all day thought it was fair that the elderly durgin, who had only brought a load of clover hay to the tallet and part of a load of their manure to the muck bury, should be allowed to nose in first like that every time.

When Blossom's son, Jolly, was five years old, a Birmingham business man came to the village buying horses for town work, pulling the drays and waggons on the cobbled streets of the city. He offered the Squire a good price for the five-year-old gelding which the Squire accepted. "I've sold Jolly for town work in Birmingham, Fred," the Squire told his carter one morning in the stable.

"No, gaffer, never, how could you?" Fred Dunn replied. "One of my best in the team."

A sad day that was for Fred Dunn as the four in line plodded up and down Beckfords Way. "I want him taken to Ashchurch station on Wednesday to go by train to Birmingham, Fred," the Squire told his carter.

"I can't take him, gaffer," Fred replied, sitting in tears on the stable bench.

"No, the boy can lead him there, he's going to a good home. He will be well fed and looked after by the Birmingham Brewery." Fred Dunn was not impressed. It was like losing a member of the family, but Jolly went to the city.

Ploughing went on and another horse took Jolly's place in the team. Every year horse ploughing left the same pattern of ridge and furrow in straight lines on Bredon hillside, lines that remained apparent in the grassland when the arable fell down to pasture, years after. Long Fred and Joe Salter ploughed the limestone hill land near the quarry with a team of oxen pulling the long wooden plough. It was here that Shepherd Peart folded off the turnips with his sheep in hurdled pens. Fred Dunn ploughed on the stronger land below with one of the new Ransome iron ploughs that were becoming popular over the country. But when spring came and the ploughland which was due for a summer fallow was to be ploughed back, Fred used the long wooden plough made years since by Thomas Archer the carpenter. A cumbersome looking wheel-less implement but favoured for ploughing back the fallow land in the spring.

Apart from breaking in horses Fred Dunn had broken in more ploughboys than he had had Christmas dinners. Boys of eleven or twelve years old who drove the team, soon became able to handle a pair of horses on the harrows when fourteen years old. At ten o'clock, bait time, they would sit in the hedge bottom with their slivers of hard cheese and the top off a cottage loaf, moistened with cider.

"I suppose you ploughboys would sit here all day if I didn't make a move," Fred Dunn used to say, as he got up off his seat on a corn sack ready to start the to and fro with the plough horses. Handling his turnip watch with a kind of reverence, he would say to his ploughboy, "'Tis half past ten, bwoy and that's what kills old horses."

"I don't understand, Fred."

"Oi, starting again, bwoy, that's what kills um."

Fred Dunn had acquired a philosophy all of his own, working Baldwyn's plough land. Day in, day out he filled his one-gallon costrel barrel with cider at six-thirty every morning, slung it with his frail basket on the harness of the foremost horse, then plodded the furrows of clay as the shield board followed the plough share and turned up that unyielding land under Bredon Hill.

The care taken by Fred Dunn with the horses was typical of the nineteenth-century carters around Bredon Hill. As the bullock teams of the hills became less common, horses were the motive power on the farms. It was vital that they should be well fed and looked after. Fred and the boy groomed all the horses after the day's work, making sure to brush and curry comb the tide mark off their sweaty shoulders, looking carefully for collar sores. Fred sent fleeces of Walter Peart's wool down to Nathan Burge, the saddler, to soften the straw-lined collars. He and the boy washed the clay from the feathery hair on their hooves after a day's ploughing on winter wet land. He stood his team in the horse pond when their hooves were cracked and dry in the summer. If a horse got griped by eating the windfall apples from the hedgerow trees, the boy walked it around until the wind went from the distended belly, while Fred drenched the animal with the usual medicine of linseed oil and turpentine.

As the acres were ploughed and harrowed, sown and reaped, one wonders how many miles Fred walked every year at the Squire's Manor Farm. The boys he trained became ploughmen themselves, setting the wheels of their ploughs for furrow depth and the hake at the beam end for furrow width, keeping up a tradition of skill and pride in their work they had learnt from Fred Dunn.

By the start of the 1860s Fred had seen the best of his life on the farm and he told Grandfather that his working days were coming to an end. "But Fred," William answered the old man, "you got a good many years to go yet. The Archdeacon lived to be ninety-six."

"Ah," Fred replied, "he lived well, and sometimes young horses die, so old ones be bound to. Whoa," he called to his team. Then he turned to the ploughboy. "Take the 'osses to the stable and get their gears off and I 'ull be along presently to give 'um their bait." The boy who sat astride the foremost horse, just clicked with his tongue and said, "Boxer, cup bwoy," in his high pitched eleven-year-old voice.

"How's that little un of your'n, William?" Fred asked with the interest of a man whose own family has grown up and married years ago.

"He's a nineter, up to everything now, and Phoebe thinks the world of him. Ah, young Jim Archer, there's no youngster like him in his mother's eyes."

"I wonder now," Fred ventured, "whether young Jim will be following the plough like me. 'Cos they tell me the land's being ploughed by steam engines over in Warwickshire."

William, who talked with the Squire almost daily at the saw pit and at the larch plantation, replied, "The Squire speaks of buying some steam tackle and he says there's talk of a railroad coming from Evesham to near Tewkesbury. The surveyors have been measuring along the side of Carrants Brook from Pecked Meadow to the Naits."

The two men speculated about how near the line would come to Carrants Field, and recalled the trouble there had been with the navvies when Mickleton tunnel was dug some years back. "But there's one thing for sure, a tunnel won't be needed to take the line along the Carrant Brook valley. Floods 'ull be the problem there," William said and the two went their separate ways.

Among the customers at the White Hart there was a lot of talk about the new railway line. "No more working all hours on the land for ten bob a week," Joe Salter said to Long Fred. "I'll get a job on the railroad."

But the older men were more doubtful about high wages coming to the village. They remembered that Mickleton tunnel and the London line employed hard working navvies from South Wales and the Black Country.

"We'll wait and see, as usual," Shepherd Peart said in his wisdom.

CHAPTER
SEVENTEEN

The Loop Line

On June 7th, 1861, that part of the loop railway line which was to run from Evesham to Ashchurch was authorised. This ten-mile stretch of railway was to become a section of track in the Barnt Green to Ashchurch branch. When complete the loop, as it was known, would be an alternative route to the main line through Bromsgrove and would bypass the steep incline over the Lickey hills.

The previous twenty years had been stormy in Gloucestershire and Worcestershire. The Cheltenham and Great Western Railway Company had run into difficulties when they constructed a line from Swindon to Kemble. Robert Gordon the Squire of Kemble, claimed £7,500 damages to his estate and also stipulated that the railway line should be taken underground near Kemble House, through an expensive four hundred and fifteen yard long tunnel, still used today. A year before, in 1840, the Birmingham and Gloucester Railway was running the other side of Bredon Hill with a station at Bredon. But the Oxford to Worcester line was bedevilled by a dispute with the contractor, and the tunnelling through the Cotswold

162

limestone at Mickleton took six years to complete by the navvies from Wales and the Black Country. While Lord Coventry insisted that Pershore station was built nearly two miles from Pershore at Pinvin, and the line was kept right away from that Georgian town.

Squire Baldwyn and Squire Holland of Dumbleton were concerned about the prospect of the loop line. They wanted a railway and had co-operated with the surveyors in choosing the route along the Carrant Valley.

There were so many little railway companies owning or leasing sections of lines, and Squire Holland of Dumbleton was in favour of the Midland Railway working our section. He knew Mr. Liddle, the Midland engineer, and wrote the following letter from his London club to his solicitor, George Badham of Tewkesbury:

> Union Club,
> Trafalgar Square,
> London.
> June 29th, 1860

Dear Sir,

I travelled up from Evesham yesterday with Mr. Liddle the Midland engineer and, from what I can learn of the determination of The Midland to fight every attempt at a line in what they call "their district", I feel more than ever inclined to doubt as to Mr. Thomas's line ever coming into existence . . . We do not care who makes the line but want a line and if Mr. Thomas's contract succeeds in obtaining the act but is left without funds for making his line our neighhourhood will be without any line for some years to come. Is Mr. Alexander Gordon the contractor, from whom Mr. Thomas has obtained small funds, requisite for taking a survey? Is not Mr. Gordon already the contractor of the Ashchurch and Malvern line? Did he not take to this line after Mr. Thomas had provided plans and drawings as an engineer? Is Mr. Thomas *now* employed as engineer by Mr. Gordon or by the contractor, whoever he is? Who has undertaken to make the Ashchurch and Malvern line and if not why is this?

I ask out of curiosity and am, dear sir,

Yours faithfully,

Edward Holland.

Tomorrow I return home to Dumbleton.

Squire Holland was wise when he doubted the power of a contractor to take on the already strong Midland Railway Company, and the engineers the Midland eventually appointed for the new line were Messrs. Liddle and Gordon. Alexander Gordon had already been involved with the contract on the Ashchurch to Malvern line through Tewkesbury and Upton on Severn.

So the Midland gave us our railway, but not before there were many disputes over the exact route it was to take through Ashton. Joseph New, who farmed the 280-acre farm north of Ashton, agreed to the line cutting through his land on certain conditions, one of which was that the contractors built a station at Ashton. The original proposal had been to build a station at Hinton on the Green and another at Beckford, missing out Ashton-under-Hill. But Mr. New insisted and the contractors had to agree. The landowners who would be involved in selling land to the Company were Squire Baldwyn, David Drinkwater, Herbert New, Joseph New, Nehemiah Cole and there was also a small farm with house, rickyard and cattle sheds to be taken into account, belonging to Hannah Abel. The solicitor for the Baldwyn estate was a Mr. Garrard of Evesham, who came out to Ashton with the story that he would like to check through the Baldwyn deeds. This he did, substituting some useless documents in their place. Using the Squire's deeds as a surety, he bought Hannah Abel's farm, thinking that the house and building and the meadows near the brook would be wanted for the route of the loop line.

The surveyors meanwhile were making sure that the railway would not be flooded by Carrants Brook. The route they settled on left Nehemiah Cole's land at Sanfield and came along the top of Joseph New's Pecked Meadow, then along west of the Naits, a pasture field that flooded in winter. Hannah Abel's farm was left 484 yards east of the proposed line and Mr. Garrard was left with a much less valuable house and holding than he had expected. Indeed, so far had he miscalculated things that he went bankrupt and when the bankruptcy court heard the case the truth came out of his fraud. He was accused of using the documents belonging to the Baldwyn family for his own and substituting worthless papers in the family chest. Grandfather told the story that the Squire proposed taking Hannah Abel's farm as payment for his loss, but Mr. Garrard had already been made bankrupt and his creditors were only paid sixpence in the pound. The Baldwyn family lost over £6,000 through Garrard's fraud.

The larch plantation had been planted, the fencing of the Manor fields was now completed, and the railway contractors offered good money to the local men who wanted work. So William Archer again left the employment of the Squire to pit his strength with the navvies from the Black Country. They were a hard working, hard drinking lot of men, men used to a roving life, used to living in the wooden huts provided by the contractors if they couldn't find better. Some found lodgings in Ashton. Fred and Martha Dunn boarded two at their cottage. Long Fred joined William as they signed on with the site foreman to start work with spades filling the carts with soil.

David Drinkwater was a contractor in a small way. For years his horses and carts had been hauling stone from the quarry on Holcombe Nap to mend the roads in Ashton village. In fact David's father had done the same through his long lifetime too. Now his son had a contract to haul the soil from the proposed railway track. The contract would last some years, for hundreds of tons of Clee Hill stone would also have to be hauled by horses from the main line station at Ashchurch to be used for ballast, forming foundations for the iron road.

Dan, who had mowed the Tewkesbury meadows years before with William Archer, joined Joe Salter working with David Drinkwater's horses.

Only Walter Peart was opposed to the new line. He told the Squire one day on the Hill as he penned his ewes, "'Tis no good, master, spoiling the best haymaking meadows by Carrants Brook. We don't need a railway, it's only five miles to Ashchurch and the main line, damn it; a five-mile walk won't hurt anybody. Now when I was in Zummerset years ago, I did walk scores of miles over the Mendips."

Squire and shepherd looked down from the Hill where horses, carts and men were cutting and carting the top soil off Didcot Ham, one of the Squire's best mowing meadows. "Never thought I'd live to zee that field being split down the middle and the soil carted away. No, gaffer, I never did."

The Squire used a telescope to watch the work; the same instrument he had used to watch his men, and his father had used to watch the making of Umberlands Lane. "Glad they are not going through William Archer's land in Carrants Field," he said to his shepherd.

"William un't averse to working along 'uth them townies," replied Walter. The Squire smiled, offering his telescope.

"No, sir, I can see enough without that contraption," his shepherd replied.

Back at home William came in from his work with the men on Didcot Ham. Mary Ann and Phoebe with baby Jim met him at the gate. "How did you like your new job then, William?" Mary enquired.

"Plenty of company of all sorts, wench, but the money's good. You fed and watered the donkey and the pig?"

"Course, bwoy," Mary replied, "and Phoebe and I have been down working in Carrants Field. I could see your yellow cord trousers as you bent with your spade over in Didcot Ham. What a noisy lot of men you are, to be sure. The Squire's mares and their foals galloped to the end of Wet Furrow standing frightened under Hill Withy hedge."

"Horses 'ull have to get used to the sound of steam engines soon," William answered as he sat down to a meal of boiled fat bacon, potatoes and swedes. After tea Spider Watchet came to catch up with the news of the railroads.

"Foreigners amongst us," he said. "The village is full of townies. One is a sweethearting along with Dan's daughter, your friend Dan, William."

"Steady chap he is, works with me," William replied, "and he's coming along with me to Chapel at Merecombe on Sunday."

"That's nice for him William, but do be careful, I've heard that some navvies are light fingered."

William looked at his clock as it ticked away towards the bedtime hour of nine o'clock. He thought, as Phoebe and Jim were safely in bed, of the days when he mowed Didcot Ham for hay. "Remember the stocking?" he said to Mary Ann. "That's filling up now with the contractors' pay."

168

"You'll need it, my bwoy now, because I've missed a fort-night and I am pretty sure there's another young Archer on the way."

William said quietly, "We'll manage somehow, but just be careful working on Carrants Field."

Spider laughed and was unable to speak for a minute, then he blurted out, "Millie's in the family way too."

William replied, "That was after the Whitsun Sport on the Hill, I reckon, 'cos the doctor always said that lots of youngsters can be dated back to that event."

Mary Ann was a bit put out by the men's casual way of talking about another birthday. "I'll go and see Millie. I shall be back by nine."

William turned the subject, saying, "Primitive Methodist that Black Country chap is. Comes from Tipton."

There is no doubt that Grandfather William Archer would never have gone to work on the new railroad had it not been for improving his chances on the rickety ladder which was the only means of lifting a man from being a labourer to the state of being, one day, wholly independent. He longed for extra acres to enable him to become a member of that select company of little master men.

David Drinkwater was in that category, and he persuaded Neal, who had worked with Dan and William, to work for him hauling to and fro the railway track. Sooner than expected the section of the new iron road was taking shape in Didcot Ham. Messrs. Liddle and Gordon, the contractors, employed more men from the Black Country. David's men with horses and carts were hauling stone, not only the hard Clee Hill stone from Ashchurch station but the soft limestone off Halcombe Nap. The navvies put a foundation on the clay of the Carrant Valley. Sand from Beckford was needed in quantity.

At the Rabbit Lane, local builders had fetched cart loads of sand for years, repairing cottages and building cow sheds. It appeared that the whole of the meadows on either side of Rabbit Lane was one huge area of sand, just a spit below the top soil. Rabbits gave away that secret when the mouths of their burrows had pure sand scratched from below the surface.

Messrs. Liddle and Gordon engaged David Drinkwater among other small contractors to haul the sand from Rabbit Lane. Ding dong, all day, Dan, Neal and Joe Salter walked the two miles from Beckford to Didcot Ham with loads of sand.

Walter Peart was upset at the state of Beckfords Way, the road they travelled. "Soon be a quagmire, sir," he told the Squire. "Used to be a decent road until this yer railroad was started. Now which way do I go with my sheep to Tewkesbury market, because they won't walk through that stony track with wheel ruts a foot deep."

"Through Grafton, then across what used to be Squire Wakeman's fields to Conderton," the Squire suggested.

Already builders were working with blue lias stone from Bidford-on-Avon on the station house at Ashton. Some of the soft stone was excavated by the navvies when they made a deep cutting near Broom.

170

The first metals and sleepers arrived. Long Fred, William and Nathan Burge, a Beckford man, were chosen among the local men to help carry the lengths of metal rails. Nathan Burge was a saddler with his brother, but he chose to work on the new line. Carrying the metal rails one day in the hot summer, William Archer walked up into some rising ground with his end of metal. A lot of weight came into his broad back and he felt something give under his broad leather belt. It was what he dreaded, a double rupture, and in those days little could be done to ease the condition. Walter Peart had suffered in the same way when he was carrying a heavy sheep trough on the Hill.

William was a sad man when he went home that evening to his wife, but Nathan Burge did offer to make him a truss. At the saddlers' at Beckford, after measuring Grandfather, Nathan made him a support from the breeching of a cart horse, and this truss supported him the rest of his life.

The summer of 1864 saw the final work done on the Ashchurch end of the new railway line. William left the employment of Liddle and Gordon, returned to the Manor and Carrants Field. But Long Fred stayed and was taken on as a permanent plate layer on the railroad.

William recalled to Dad how the Squire, Joseph New and Nehemiah Cole, whose land adjoined the new track, fenced the small paddocks of pasture near the line all ready to put the horses down there to familiarise them with the hiss of the steam engines and the smoke

171

from the funnels, apart from the rattle of goods waggons.

It was on October 1st 1864 when the line was opened to both passenger and goods traffic. Squire Baldwyn and David Drinkwater organised a grand feast in the Groaten Field to celebrate the great day. William, Fred Dunn, Neal, Dan, Long Fred and Joe Salter were working for some days before under the guidance of old Jim Dance. Horse jumps were erected; the field was marked out for races by the boys and girls; Union Jack flags hung from larch poles; trestle tables were weighed down with great joints of beef.

Spider Watchet killed four strong pork pigs for Tilda Dance, Martha, Lotty and Mary Ann to cook in the big Manor kitchen, for the Ashton folk to eat at the dinner. Dinner was held at one o'clock, then came the races, the horse jumping by local farmers, dog races, a parade of the hounds, shin kicking by the local lads, watched with a critical eye by William Archer, once the champion of Bredon Hill.

Before the bonfire was lit and when the hogsheads of cider were running low, Squire Baldwyn had a ceremony to perform. "You all know, I'm sure," he told the villagers, "that had it not been for Joseph New, my good neighbour, the parish would not have had a railway station. It's my pleasure to present this Georgian silver tankard to him today, which is given by the people of this village thanking him." The cup presented bore this inscription:

Presented to Joseph New of Ashton by his friends and neighbours for his successful exertions in obtaining a railway station in the parish 1864.

As the first trains puffed along the Carrant Valley, cattle and sheep in the field bunched up under the hedges and trees, afraid of the black engines and coloured carriages, and of the steam and smoke of the monsters they would have to live with. Fred Dunn took the Squire's horses, and Jim Dance the hunters, down to graze the paddocks beside the new railway track. As Jim Dance said to David Drinkwater, "These horses, whether cart horses or hunters, will have to meet the trains at the station and crossing the Groaten Bridge."

David Drinkwater had not got a field near the railway but he arranged with the Squire to take his horses to one of the paddocks. "You have got your railway, but what about the Beckford Road. Almost impassable since the carts hauled the sand, sir."

Walter Peart's words were remembered by the Squire who called a Vestry Meeting to discuss the matter. The Minutes read as follows:

A Vestry Meeting, March 24th, 1865 at St. Barbara's Church, Ashton-under-Hill
Whereas at a Parish Vestry held on the above date the purpose of which is to consider the damage done in the transition of materials through our Parish for the necessary appliances in the construction of yards and approaches at Ashton Station and near here. We estimate the damage at the sum of £160.

Persons Present:

David Drinkwater	Church Warden
John Heming	Church Warden
Joseph New	Way Warden
Thos. Baldwyn	Way Warden
William Baldwyn	Chairman
Rev. Joseph Harrison.	

So the Midland Railway Gloucester loop line was established here and soon the station became a hive of activity. A coal wharf was started. Railway trucks were loaded with the corn and the fruit from the farms and, most important, passengers travelled to towns they had never seen.

One Ashton man who had been working at Beckford, two miles away, had always walked home from work in the evening. But one night he decided to take the train instead, and arrived at Ashton station with his ticket. The porter in charge of the station called, "Tickets, please."

The workman replied, "I paid for this bit of paste board at Beckford. I'm keeping it, that's mine."

CHAPTER
EIGHTEEN

Change at Ashchurch

After the excitement and the novelty, the jobs and the convenience — and the inconvenience — the loop line had brought to Ashton, village life returned to its usual undisturbed pace and pattern. William Archer and Mary Ann's family was increasing, first by Polly and Lucy, and then by baby George. It was just before Michaelmas of the year George was born when the Rev. Joseph Harrison received a letter from a vicar he knew in Cheltenham, asking him to recommend a strong country girl of good character as a maid of all work for one of his parishioners in the more select part of that town. The vicar immediately thought of Phoebe Archer. William Archer had a lot of mouths to feed now and Phoebe had grown into a sensible girl. What was more, since leaving the vestry school she had been regular at church service, despite her father's leaning towards the Methodist connection at Merecombe. So the Rev. Harrison rode his horse over to Carrants Field and found William busy lifting his potato crop. "Surely you don't want the Lady Day rent yet awhile, Master Harrison?" Grandfather asked his parson landlord. He had paid the Michaelmas rent in July.

"No, William, but how about a tot of your rhubarb wine in the hovel while we talk business."

"Come in, sir, but what is the business?" William opened the door of his shed.

"One of the fine houses at Pittville in Cheltenham needs a young girl to live in as one of the maids. I know the house. It's a fine place near Pittville lake, and there is a God-fearing housekeeper over the girls."

William supped the wine and looked across his land to the willow-lined brook and the Hill beyond. "I don't know what to say, sir, 'cause I had it in mind that Phoebe should go to service at a farmer's house in the country." He paused a while then said, "Cheltenham, 'tis full of the idle rich. Some men I'm told 'ull take advantage of a country wench."

"She'll be all right in Pittville," the Vicar replied. "And I'll give her a reference."

That evening William, Mary Ann and Phoebe talked over the Vicar's offer. Phoebe was anxious to go to Cheltenham; she said Mr. Dance, the Squire's groom, said it was a fine place with a tree-lined promenade and that King George III had gone there to drink the spa waters.

"Better water flows from Bredon Hill out of Paris Gardens," William replied.

Mary Ann thought she should take the post. So the Rev. Harrison was informed and he arranged for her to go at Michaelmas weekend.

"I'm not taking her in my donkey cart," William warned. "Eleven miles is too far for Ned, and besides it won't look right somehow in Pittville."

So Mary Ann persuaded her husband to ask young David Drinkwater, old David's son, if he might be going Cheltenham way about his own business and if he would take their daughter, and young David was more than willing to show off his brand new turn-out — a sprung trap and a chestnut mare with silver-mounted harness. David had done a spell in the Yeomanry and fancied himself with both young horses and young women.

The morning came when Phoebe was to leave the village for the town. Mary Ann packed a tin box, making sure to include her daughter's brush and comb, her Bible and prayer book and some paper to write home on. Dressed in her black frock with lace collar, white bonnet, black stockings and black buttoned boots, Phoebe waited nervously for young David. "Mind you speak respectfully to young Master Drinkwater," Mary Ann warned her daughter, and went on to remind her yet again to read her Bible and not forget her prayers.

The excitement of bowling along in a fine trap with a dashing young man beside her quite overcame Phoebe's first pangs of homesickness. As they sped past the Pittville Pump Room and the tree-lined gardens of the town, she noticed the polished brass lamps on the trap.

"It must be a wonderful thing driving a horse like this at night time," she ventured.

David smiled and replied airily that when you had ridden in the Yeomanry this sort of driving was really nothing. Most evening dances, he added, were arranged when the moon is full. Phoebe wondered if she would ever get the chance to go to dances in Cheltenham, but said nothing. When the fine Mr. Drinkwater and his turn-out arrived at Pittville, the gardener from the house carried Phoebe's modest tin box up to the room she was to share with another young maid.

Ellen, her room mate, was fourteen years old. She had been in service there for over a year. "How far have you come, Phoebe?" she said as she showed her where to hang her belongings.

"Oh, must be over ten miles. It took Mr. Drinkwater over an hour. I've never been so far before, only to Evesham with Dad, that's five miles."

Ellen laughed, "I come from near Derby. Came by train, I did."

Soon the housekeeper set Phoebe to work cleaning and scrubbing passages and rooms that seemed to her like working in the Queen's palace. Up at six o'clock every morning, Phoebe collected the boots and shoes and cleaned them and carried hot water to the bedrooms for the lady and gentleman of the house to wash. Visitors came down from London and she had difficulty in understanding some things they said, but tried her best not to speak broad Gloucestershire but as the Rev. Harrison did in church.

Phoebe and Ellen saw little of the mistress, as they called her, but addressed her as "Ma'am" when they did occasionally meet. The housekeeper, Miss Evans from Cardiff, ran the house and she sent them off to church on Sunday. The Church of Holy Apostles was half a mile from Pittville, very modern compared with

St. Barbara's at Ashton. The worshippers, top hatted
gentlemen and crinolined ladies, turned up in shining
horsedrawn carriages. Their pews were near the chancel
steps, but Phoebe and Ellen were told to sit near the
font towards the back of the church. Phoebe thought
the organ was beautiful, so different from the little
harmonium at St. Barbara's. Back at Pittville the
housekeeper would ask the girls the text preached that
morning. "Some weeks you will attend at Evensong and
I will go to Morning Prayer, but Ellen will explain that
to you, Phoebe."

After work all day, Phoebe and Ellen had a little
while to read before bed time. Miss Evans gave them
suitable books and Phoebe was overwhelmed by the
light of the gas lamps, so bright after her dad's oil lamp.

David Drinkwater went to Cheltenham with his pony
trap every week and after a month, when Phoebe had
written home, he arranged to take her back to Ashton
to stay overnight at her parents'. Her letters had been
cheerful but she always sent her love to Jim and the rest
of her brothers and sisters, and to Neddy the donkey.
The housekeeper, Miss Evans, told Phoebe that she
would have to be back at work the following lunch
time. "You can come on the train," she said.

As David Drinkwater's pony trotted up the
wheel-rutted road, Ashton village mothers and their
children waved when they saw Phoebe coming home.
Millie Watchet was there with Mary Ann to greet the
young housemaid. That evening by the late autumn
fireside Phoebe told her parents and the family all
about Cheltenham. She had bought some sweets for

the children, a handkerchief for her mother, and a walking stick for William, her dad. "The streets, Dad," she said, "are lit by gas. So carriages can go along them late at night to balls at the Town Hall and plays at the Opera House. It's wonderful."

William Archer spoke up sharply to his daughter, "Now theatres and dances are the Devil's work and I hope you'll never have time for such places. I always had my doubts about Cheltenham," he added.

When Joseph Harrison heard what William said, he jokingly remarked, "William speaks like another Cobbett."

"I've got to go back by train tomorrow to be at Pittville by lunch time."

"There's the ten past eight to Ashchurch then change, that will be in Cheltenham in time," Mary Ann told her daughter.

"You go with her, Mother. She's never been by train and I'll run you down to the station with the donkey cart."

It was about seven forty-five when William took his wife and daughter to the new station at Ashton-under-Hill. Phoebe and her mother changed trains at Ashchurch and took the main line train from Birmingham. "'Tis going all the way to Bristol, Mother," Phoebe said as they joined a full compartment of passengers at Ashchurch junction. Mary Ann took the next train back from Cheltenham station while her daughter walked to her employer's house at Pittville.

180

The winter passed slowly for William without the company of his daughter Phoebe. It seemed that Phoebe to him was like the ewe lamb he had learnt about at the Merecombe Methodist meeting. Strict, protective, but kind, Grandfather was to his children.

The letters from Phoebe came from Cheltenham quite regularly. Mary Ann read them out to her husband who never grasped the mystery of the printed word.

The spring in Pittville gardens with the yellow of thousands of daffodils and the various coloured tulips was so different from the wallflowered gardens of Ashton. "Ellen has invited me to Derbyshire for a weekend, Easter time. Miss Evans says we can go and I've saved my pocket money for the train fare."

So read Phoebe's letter one March morning. "I don't know, Derbyshire," William said to his wife. "I suppose she will have to go."

Mary Ann nodded as she sat by the fire reading her Bible. The weekend arrived. The two girls took the through train to Birmingham New Street, then changed for Derby.

Ellen's father met them at the station with his horse and spring cart and took them to a village five miles away where he had a little farm. Phoebe liked the old farm house and enjoyed the bacon for breakfast which tasted like bacon at home. At dinner, when the Yorkshire pudding came alone on the plate, swimming in gravy, she wondered what would come after, but the beef and potatoes and greens were to her liking.

The view from the house up on a hill was of the Peak District, which Ellen said was beautiful, while towards the Nottingham border Phoebe saw the great wheels above the coal pits where the men came home from work as black as the tom cat at home.

"'Tis chapel tonight, girls," Ellen's father announced on the Sunday morning. In the little village chapel it reminded Phoebe of Merecombe where her dad worshipped. The choir sang heartily but Phoebe had difficulty in understanding the words. The piece where they sang "Jesus of Nazareth Passeth By" sounded to her like "Jesus of Nazareth Parsnip Wine". She told her dad, William, that when next she was home, but William admitted that the folk from away "do speak different", but told Phoebe he hoped she would never speak profanely about anything from the Scriptures.

So Phoebe, working in Cheltenham and coming home on days off to Ashton, learnt the art of housework and got used to travelling by train.

She was not the only person from Ashton who got into the way of travel. Squire Baldwyn had not been a man to shift far until his village became a link on the Midland Railway network. But now the branch line joined the main line at Ashchurch junction and from there it was easy to travel to most of the chief towns and cities in England.

His neighbour, young David Drinkwater, persuaded Squire William to go with him to the main agricultural shows of the day. It was at these shows they first saw the early agricultural ploughing engines. These steam engines fascinated the Squire. The huge deep digging ploughs were already being used by Mr. Bomford over in Warwickshire.

"I'd like a set of that tackle," the Squire said to David as they both admired the engines ploughing a demonstration field at the show.

Like his father, and *his* father before him, David was a small yeoman farmer who could be chiefly called a dog and stick man; cattle, sheep and pigs were his main concern. "Well, William," David replied, "get yourself an engine and I have got the right man in mind as your driver."

"Who, to be sure?" the Squire said with his usual chuckle. "Not Fred Dunn, nor Spider or Joe Salter, they are horse and cattle men."

"Man off the railroad. I'm thinking of one," David ventured.

"Not William Archer, for he and his brother George work their Carrants Field when not working for me."

"How about Long Fred? He's employed as a fireman at Ashchurch station now and he does drive the Gloucester Express Goods," David informed the Squire. "But make it worth his while, and buy an engine. I know Long Fred hankers to get back on the land."

Taylor's coal wharf at Beckford station was busy those days supplying house coal to the farms around the Hill, and steam coal to the few steam traction engines. As their train drew into Beckford David turned to his friend and said, "That's the coal to fire the traction engines. It's hard steam coal from Wales and

183

Bomford's are growing record crops of corn after steam ploughing at Bevington."

On their way to a show near Worcester, the Squire and David were walking down the Foregate Street in that city, after lunch at the Hop Market Hotel, when under the bridge near the station came a steam traction engine on its way to the show. It thundered over the cobbled street, pulling a plough and towing a black wooden caravan on iron wheels.

The brasses on the front of the engine compared quite well with the martingales on a well-groomed horse. The mixture of polished brass and black boiler were contrasted only by the painted wheels of the engine. "Stop," William called to the driver, holding up his hand. "Going to the show?"

"Yes, sir, I am," the man in the peaked cap and overalls answered.

"How much?" the Squire asked bluntly.

" 'Tis for sale but I must take it to the show first," the surprised engine driver replied. From his cab he took out a book with the price of the whole outfit printed in, and, showing it to the Squire, told him that was the figure he wanted new from the works. The Squire handed him his address and told him to deliver it to Ashton after the show.

Some days after, a traction engine, plough and caravan pulled into the yard in front of the tythe barn and that is how the Squire bought his first steam engine to come into the village.

As William Archer and Long Fred walked past the Manor on the Sunday afternoon, they heard the Squire call from the summer house in his front garden, "I want a word with you."

William nudged Long Fred, saying, "He wants you to drive the traction engine, so David Drinkwater has said."

"Come with me, you fellas," and the three men walked to the tythe court. "There's a beauty," William and Long Fred heard the Squire say as he mounted the footplate of the engine.

"Ah, tidy job, but it don't compare with the engine which pulls the Gloucester Express Goods," Long Fred replied.

"Now, Fred, I want you to drive this ploughing engine if you will, and I'll pay you a sovereign a week."

"I'll do it for twenty-five shillings, sir," Long Fred countered.

"Done," the Squire said. "You are the first driver of my black horse. Give your notice to the company and we'll show the neighbourhood how to plough."

Long Fred was instructed by an engineer from the makers how to use the first steam cultivating engine. The early system of ploughing with one engine required the use of an anchored pulley on the opposite headland to the engine. The pulley paid out the steel rope while the engine winched the heavy plough across the fields. At the same time it paid out a second length of steel rope to take the plough on its return journey. The Squire found this a clumsy way to plough his fields, so he purchased another engine to stand on the opposite headland, enabling one engine to pull the plough one way and the other engine to pull the return journey. These two engines, which he called his black horses, were his pride and joy. Folk came from the villages around to see Long Fred and his engine. Spider Watchet rode on the plough, and steered across the winter stubbles. Between them they ploughed the big fields on the estate, Cinder Meadow, the Thurness, the Dean, Beckfords Way, Empits — all fields suitable for the bigger tackle.

Other changes were taking place on the estate. Jim Dance was getting old and rheumaticky, so the Squire had promoted Tilda Dance's boy, Joe, to be his groom. It was the obvious thing to do as, though he was only Jim Dance's stepson, Joe Salter seemed to have absorbed much of the older man's wisdom about horse flesh and its ways. He was also a bit of a racing man, was Joe Salter.

Meanwhile, William Archer's family were growing up. Phoebe was still in Cheltenham, Jim was in the fourth standard at the new school, Polly and Lucy were at school, while young George had a new baby sister to order about, called Emma. Then Mary Ann gave birth to her last child, my dad, in 1876.

Phoebe continued to come home from Cheltenham on the seven-forty train at Ashton when she had time off. How the younger children looked forward to her footsteps along the path past the donkey stable at Grandfather's house, and she would bring with her presents of food, cakes, sweets and clothes, given to her by her good employer in the town. She graduated from the scullery to become lady's maid to the Mayoress of Cheltenham. This gave her the opportunity to meet others in the same position, as she attended functions with the Mayoress. Phoebe became a legend to Jim, Polly, Lucy, George, Emma and later on to Tom, my dad.

Squire Baldwyn never married, living a somewhat lonely life at the Manor, looked after by his housekeeper. His father, Henry Baldwyn, had been dead a number of years and Squire William, that spare little man, tweedy, with gaiters over his spindly legs, was getting old by Victorian standards. He became obsessed with his steam engines, buying another small engine to do his threshing and for turning a saw bench in Tythe Court saw pit.

"I want that boy of yours, William, and young Henry Watchet, to clean my engines," he announced to Grandfather one winter's day.

"But they be at school, sir, nowadays, both boys," William replied.

"I need them on Monday," the Squire answered with authority.

So Jim Archer and Henry Watchet were employed at seven-pence per day cleaning the Squire's engines, with oily rags and polish for the brass. The school, opened in 1877, ruled that any child over ten years of age who could be beneficially employed at work should be exempt from attendance the whole time, but would be required to attend one hundred and fifty times per year at three pence per head, per week; so the Squire was within his rights when he employed Jim and Henry polishing the engines. And in return for the loving care he lavished on them the steam engines of Squire Baldwyn rewarded him with better crops of corn and helped to drain the heavy Vale land.

CHAPTER
NINETEEN

Barton Fair

The start of 1879 struck a crippling blow at Squire Baldwyn's sheep on Bredon Hill. Shepherd Peart noticed his Cotswold ewes beginning to lose condition round Christmas. Heavy in lamb, they developed a listless look, their jaws were swollen, their eyes glassy. It was the fluke again, perhaps to be expected after an exceptionally wet season. That lambing time Bredon Hill was strewn with the carcasses of ewes. Some had lambed and lost their lambs. Others were too weak to lamb as they died, their livers riddled with the fluke grub. This was the Squire's first major financial catastrophe and he lost most of his flock.

"No more sheep for me, William," he told Grandfather when he rode down to see him at Carrants Field.

"What's to become of Walter Peart, then?" William Archer asked.

"I'm going to breed horses on the Hill," replied the Squire, "and he is going to help to look after them instead."

Once he had made up his mind about the horses, Squire Baldwyn could barely contain his impatience until Michaelmas and the day of the great Barton Fair which was held every year at that time in the city of Gloucester. Sheep were on offer from the Welsh hills, cattle from the Severn Vale, but, most important, it was a horse fair. The Squire took David Drinkwater with him on the eight-ten a.m. train from Ashton station.

"If you buy a good bunch of yearlings at Gloucester, how do you propose getting them home?" David asked, as they waited for the main line train at Ashchurch junction.

"Spider Watchet and young Jim Archer are coming down on the mid-day train. They'll meet us at the Spread Eagle Hotel and drive the horses along the Tewkesbury road," explained the Squire.

"How about fodder, William?"

"That wiry tough grass on Spring Hill will feed them through the winter, and the clover rich near Great Hill Barn will fill their bellies when the snow covers the knolp by the beeches and the quarry. Besides, the old barn will shelter a good number when the weather's unkind." The Squire had worked out all the answers to doubters, so David held his peace, not wanting to annoy his more powerful neighbour.

At the market, the broken-in four- and five-year-olds were tied up with their blue, red and cream coloured halters to the railings of the market place. The cart colts and fillies were standing tightly together in the iron-fenced pens. Welsh ponies, cobs and smaller animals were herded together under the trees, impounded by boys and youths with whips.

The sale of the horses was to be done partly by auction and partly by private dealing. Everywhere horse copers, farmers and drovers walked the cobbled alleys between the pens with long whips. In the road by the Wessex Hotel, men, dwarfed by their giant charges, trotted great shire horses, five-year-olds, fit for town work. The dealers who were buying for the city brewers bent their backs and looked carefully at the action of the hind legs to be sure legs and hooves were in order. If the hooves were too close together and the animal trotted in a hen-toed fashion, it was useless for town work. The copers ran their professional hands down the legs looking for spavins, grease, ring bones and the like. Grasping their fetlocks, they examined the frog of the hoof looking for any defects there.

As the carter held the halter, the dealers mouthed the animals, counting and checking their teeth for age. Another coper's trick was to clench the fist and make as if to punch the horse in the brisket to see if the animal was a roarer. If it made a roaring noise, that meant there was a defect in its wind and it could be broken winded.

Squire Baldwyn and David Drinkwater were not interested in the merits of five-year-olds that day. After a drink at the Spread Eagle they spent half an hour around the cheap jack stalls listening to the medicine men who boiled kettles of water on paraffin stoves and brewed secret herbs for curing all ills to be sampled by all and sundry. They watched with interest the man who cut the leather laces for the farm workers' boots from a sheet of leather with a sharp knife, keeping up a constant patter of talk on politics and religion.

See Quar, the coloured man, had a whole ring of folk watching him as he drew bad teeth from the simple country folk, while his assistant beat on a drum to hide any cries of pain. He also manipulated arthritic limbs, seating the sufferer in a kind of dentist's chair as he rubbed in strong-smelling potions and massaged them with the secrets of the East. Men lame with corns took off their hob-nailed boots for See Quar to uproot them.

So, past the sweet and gingerbread stalls, William and David came to look at a pen of ten colts, all from a well-known shire horse breeder.

"Twenty-four pound a piece, sir," the owner asked William. "Make some honest workers one day."

As if he could see the money burning a hole in the Squire's pocket, the man held out his hand to clasp a deal on the spot, but David hastily took his friend aside for a moment. "Shall I deal with him, William," he whispered.

"Ah, all right," the Squire replied.

"Not a lot of grass keep about this autumn, ya know," David said, "and twenty-four pound's a lot to pay for yearlings."

"A good lot of colts. They all thrive. Look how well ribbed up they are after a summer on the rough common at Shuthunger. Not a bad one among them," the owner answered.

David climbed the railings and with his cane looked the bunch over. "You are right, sir, a useful lot and worth the money, but after a dry summer if the grass grows now the frost will level it by St. Luke's Day. Worth the money they would be if the autumn was favourable. Eighteen pound a piece is our price," David stated.

"No, no, can't be done. I'd rather take 'um home, sir," the farmer replied.

He had ten more colts in the next pen, a level similar lot. "Take the two pens, all twenty of them, at twenty-two pound a piece," he quoted David.

David took the Squire aside, "How about the two pens if they will come at twenty pound?" he said quietly.

"Ah, yes, I'd like them. Have a go."

"Twenty pound apiece, and that's buying them at a good price, but my friend happens to have keep on Bredon Hill. I'd say eighteen pound is their value," David told the farmer.

"Make it guineas," the farmer replied. "Give us your hand."

"Sorry, we'll have to look elsewhere," David said looking down on the ground as if that was final. "Come on, William, plenty to pick from today," he said holding the Squire's arm and walking away.

The farmer called them back. "At twenty pound apiece they can be yours. But it's daylight robbery," he added, for all to hear.

"Give him your hand, William, if you're satisfied," said David, and as the men clasped hands the farmer shouted, "Sold".

So twenty yearlings were destined for Bredon Hill.

Barton Fair was also a hiring fair. The carters who wanted a year's work on a farm and live in, wore horse-hair in their caps or hats, the shepherds sheep's wool, the cowmen a little cow-hair in the button-hole, and some servant girls carried mops. "Do you need a good man for your horses, sir," an eighteen-year-old, strong-looking chap asked the Squire.

David Drinkwater turned to his neighbour saying, "Fred Dunn's getting past it, you know. He won't work for ever. Shall I ask this fellow about himself?"

The Squire agreed. Meanwhile the farmer from Shuthunger Common told the Ashton men that this fellow who was a Welshman from Brecon had worked a year for his brother at Tewkesbury and a very good worker he was.

"Meet me in the Spread Eagle, and take this shilling. I'll find you work at Ashton," the Squire promised.

"How do I find your farm, sir?"

"You will help my men to drive these colts back home. They will be in the Spread Eagle at two o'clock."

"What's your name?" David asked.

"Always known as Taffy Price," was the reply.

At the Spread Eagle, Uncle Jim and Spider arrived to drink their beer and eat their beef with Taffy before starting back with the colts for Ashton. The Squire told them to drive the colts to the Odessa Inn the Gloucester side of Tewkesbury for the night. The inn was kept by one of the Squire's cousins, and had a two-acre paddock attached. They reached it with their bunch of yearlings at dusk and drove them on to Spring Hill the following day.

"The last train to Ashton leaves about a quarter to seven, William," David reminded the Squire as they were eating and drinking at The Monk's Retreat, that ancient inn where the music and dancing continued until the late hours.

"We'll go back in the morning, there's nothing spoiling at Ashton," replied the Squire, who by now was getting what David Drinkwater described as "market peart". "Two beds for the night, landlord," he ordered, "and fill up the pewters all round."

"Saved you four pound a piece on the colts," David reminded William, adding, "It doesn't do to be so free with your money. These horsemen try it on thinking that we countrymen are easily had."

"Sure enough," William replied, "then perhaps another year I might consider selling some horses here and leave you to do the arguing."

"A pleasure to do that for a friend," David replied, and the couple sat in the smoke room listening to the German band playing, while a dancing bear performed in the public bar.

"Remember William Archer's bear in the pigsty," the Squire said with a smile. "Young Jim is the dead spit of his father, broad shoulders and that pair of bushy eyebrows. I suppose they got my colts as far as the Odessa," he added with the careless rapture of a gentleman relaxed by drink.

Next morning Joe Salter met the twelve-twenty train at Ashton station with a pony and trap, hoping that the two men would arrive. As they drove up the Groaten towards the Manor, Spider Watchet, Jim Archer and

Taffy Price were driving the bunch of colts up through Tythe Court towards Paris Hill to the Spring Hill rough pasture.

Never one to do things by halves, the Squire took David Drinkwater to the Barton Fair the following year and bought twenty-five shire mares in foal and a shire stallion. This scheme of the Squire's was a sound one, for the foals would surely grow into money. This time the horses were sent from Gloucester by train and Uncle Jim remembered the scene as the horse boxes arrived for unloading at Beckford station. Fred Dunn, Walter Peart, Spider and Joe Salter met the train. They haltered the horses, mostly young fillies, in lines of six and walked with them along the Beckfords Way to Ashton.

There were black mares, bay mares, chestnuts, dapple greys — the finest lot of shires seen in the neighbourhood when they were all together in Boss Close or Church Close. And when foaling time came at the Manor the following May, there was the prettiest sight of horse flesh ever in the spring sunshine. Slick as oonts, that's moles, was Grandfather's description of the Squire's mares.

Uncle Jim worked with some of these mares, driving for the ploughman, Fred Dunn. The foals played in the ploughed fields while their mothers worked, and they suckled before the day's work started and after it finished.

There were several mares that failed to foal in May. The Squire stabled them in the nag stable and Joe

196

Salter examined them. "Oh, they're in foal, sir," was his conclusion, "and when the apple's ripe it 'ull fall."

Uncle Jim rose from being ploughboy to be under cowman for the Squire, milking the Shorthorns at the Manor. After a couple of years, the Squire did so well with his colts and fillies which David Drinkwater sold for him at the Barton Fair that he bought a couple of thoroughbred yearlings from one of the sales of bloodstock, and that set his interest in horseflesh off on quite a different tack.

CHAPTER
TWENTY

Fly by Night

One of Squire Baldwyn's thoroughbred yearlings was a bay, the other jet black with a white diamond flash on its forehead. He called this one Fly By Night and it looked clearly the more promising of the two youngsters from the start.

"Should be backed now," Joe Salter told his master. "Needs a little work."

"Take young Jim Archer up to the racecourse on top of the Hill then, and between you give both of them a try-out," Squire Baldwyn told his groom.

Jim Archer and the groom began by spending some days handling the horses in Ten Furlongs, a grass field usually grazed by the Squire's milking cows. They found Fly By Night a good-tempered animal, but the bay was awkward. Joe seated Uncle Jim on Fly By Night, while he held him on a leading rein, circling Ten Furlongs enough times each day to make the young animal all of a lather with sweat.

When they did get up those nine hundred feet on Bredon summit to the racecourse it was a lovely day in May. They were alone in the world of peewits and the incessant song of skylarks. Away to the east, the

198

Cotswolds were screened by a row of fir trees above the badger setts. The racecourse was marked out by furze-thatched fencing which followed the line of the stone walls around four big fields some ten yards in, thus forming a green road from start to finish. Joe Salter and Uncle Jim schooled Fly By Night round this track all that season. When he was satisfied, the groom went to the Squire.

"I want you to come up the Hill and see young Jim ride that horse of yours, sir, for I reckon 'tis a outstanding animal you have got."

So the Squire rode up past Paris through the Leasows to Spring Hill, then through the bridle gate to the racecourse behind Grafton Firs.

"Now, Jim, show your mettle," Joe ordered Uncle, and Jim rode Fly By Night like a veteran around the Hill.

"What about the bay?" the Squire said when he saw the other horse tied to a hawthorn tree under the wall.

"Un't worth a hatful of crabs," Joe Salter answered, "but you have got a winner here, sir," stroking Fly By Night and telling Uncle to dismount.

That evening the Squire was up at Orchard Farm, the home of David Drinkwater. Round the stone open fireplace they drank a glass of wine and smoked their long churchwarden pipes; pipes all farmers and landowners kept for visiting friends. They were marked by name in a wicker basket.

"Got a useful horse, so Tilda Dance's boy reckons, but we can't train for racing on the Hill."

David replied, "No, William, you have had some good hunters, point-to-pointers, but with a thoroughbred that's a different card trump. Take him to Mr. Davies's stable at Woolas Hall. He trains some winners. That's if you want him to win big races."

The Squire rode over the Hill next day and fixed up with Mr. Davies to train Fly By Night. Uncle Jim rode the horse to the Davies's stables. Then he and Joe Salter together got the awkward bay into some sort of shape. "He's as awkward as a tup," the groom said, adding, "while Fly By Night's as sensible as a Christian."

Mr. Davies sent word over to the Manor that Fly By Night had finished his training and was fit for the racecourse. The Squire entered him for the Craven meeting. He won his race well, then ran a close second at York, ridden by J. Watts. The Squire was advised against running him in the Derby, knowing that he would have no chance against Persimmon. But the Prix du Jockey Club was to be run as usual at Chantilly in France and many considered that to be the French Derby. "Have a go with him," Mr. Davies persuaded the Squire.

Squire Baldwyn recalled how his family had come to England from France five hundred years before and built the hamlet they had called Paris above his Manor on Bredon Hill, and he thought he might like to go and race Fly By Night in the land of his forefathers. The Rev. Joseph Harrison and David Drinkwater would go too. So the Squire entered international racing circles and all the Hill villages hung on news of the outcome.

The bookmakers priced Fly By Night at twenty to one against when he entered the betting. Squire Baldwyn and the Rev. Harrison were each said to have wagered £500 on him at this price and congratulated each other on their early bet when the odds shortened the morning of the race.

William Archer, his brother George, and Spider were in the White Hart on the Saturday evening before the race on Sunday. Joe Salter came in all excited, confident Fly By Night was a certainty to win. But Walter Peart over his quart pot of cider warned, "They won't let a nondescript animal win over in France."

"I'll bet a sovereign that Fly By Night will win by a distance," Spider blurted out from his corner of the settle, more to annoy Shepherd Peart than anything else.

"You talk as your belly guides you, Spider, but I'll take you on with that gamble."

"Allus was a bit wild, you were, Spider, like your old Dad was at the Enclosure," Long Fred said from the doorway where he was drinking his first pint of cider.

"Runs in families then does it, like wooden legs?" Spider replied.

"The Squire, David Drinkwater and the Rev. Harrison be all gone to France to see the race. Gone yesterday to Dover, so they say," William Archer told his friends.

"They be running at Shan't Tilly," George Archer ventured.

"Don't pronounce it like that, I'm sure," Long Fred said.

"We got to ring the bells when Fly By Night has won that race," Spider said, "and there's going to be a do of some sort in the ballroom."

"What ballroom?" Shepherd Peart spluttered, almost choking with the sharp cider. "What ballroom?"

"The new granary over the nag stables. Have dances, parties and balls some Saturday nights and Joe Salter makes a few ha'pence from the folks he stables the horses for."

Joe Salter turned on Spider Watchet. "Mind thee own business, Spider. Some folks grow tall, others grow up. Thee hast done neither."

Over in Chantilly next day the race was run at a cracking pace with Fly By Night leading the field all the way, but towards the post he was beaten into fourth place by a French horse. It was with some disappointment the Ashton party returned to England. How much the Squire had staked on Fly By Night, or his parson companion, the Rev. Harrison, has been a debatable point in the village since that fateful day. Joseph Harrison borrowed money off Grandfather to live on for six months but paid him back. Squire Baldwyn became a recluse for a year and peeped behind the curtained windows of the Manor. "No heart to come out," Uncle Jim said.

Until one day, when Long Fred was threshing with the portable engine at the Cross Barn. It was bait time, the men were eating bread and cheese sitting on the sacks of corn. "Get those wheels moving, Fred," the Squire called as he appeared like a ghost from behind the double doors of the barn.

"Right, sir," Long Fred replied, opening the regulator to make the huge fly wheel rotate and the belt drive the threshing machine. Away across the orchard, past the moat pond went the low-spirited Squire Baldwyn. A shadow of his former self when he dealt with all the corn merchants, cattle and horse dealers of the county. Meeting William Archer by the duck pond he harked back to the lost horserace in France. "Have you ever backed a horse, William?" he said.

"Only once, sir, in Evesham," William replied.

"But there's no racecourse in Evesham."

"I backed one into a shop window, sir, after taking some of your corn to the mill."

The Squire laughed for the first time for months and made up his mind to do as he had done before, manage the work in the farm and not leave it to his men. So he came out of his hiding and was seen on the farm not only in the day, but on moonlight nights up on Bredon Hill as well, becoming the most inoffensive, the most kindly eccentric ever to live in the parish.

The Squire kept all the old men who had worked for his father in employment on the farm. "I've had the best from you and I'll have the worst," he told his men who came, some on two sticks, to look for work.

Another mark of his growing eccentricity was that though he went on breeding horses, he stopped selling them, so that in time Bredon Hill was as much alive with horses as it was with rabbits, and Spring Hill was thick with summer mushrooms, for there's nothing like horse manure to encourage mushrooms.

The horses on the Hill had increased in such numbers that Walter Peart and Joe Salter were in a quandary how to winter them. The Squire bought waggon loads of trussed hay to feed them.

"Going to sell some yearlings at Barton Fair?" Shepherd Peart would enquire hopefully of his master.

"No, Walter, not this year," would be the reply.

Walter would look concerned. "We be overstocked on the Hill, sir."

"Now look here, Walter," the Squire said once with a smile, "I know without you telling me there are horses on Spring Hill seven years old that have never been broken in, never had a collar and bridle on, but I like to see them about. Are you satisfied?"

Come Evesham Candlemas Fair, the Squire took the eight-fifty train from Ashton station and his men, in fact most of the village, feared the worst. They knew what would happen when he saw some of the best shire horses in the West Midlands paraded down Evesham High Street. And they were right. He bought first one, then another, then a bunch of colts. The price seemed immaterial to him if he fancied an animal, so the dealers, horse copers, farmers ran him up and made him pay well over the odds.

When his men had driven the new horses along Cheltenham road and left them overnight in Pecked Meadow, the field adjoining the Umberlands Lane, they knew that winter was turning to spring and soon the Hill would be green again, but the village had become a ranch of shire horses. So life went on at the Manor and the farming dwindled in the mid-1880s. On the arable Long Fred still ploughed deep and straight with the steaming black horses. The corn crops were good, but the hay was fed to the unbroken horses on the Hill.

CHAPTER
TWENTY-ONE

The End of a Century

The Golden Jubilee of 1887 was celebrated in the village by a feast in the great barn at the Manor.

The Squire and David Drinkwater arranged the programme, or, it's most correct to say, David Drinkwater himself with the help of the Squire, who by now had become a man living in dream land. The world of fantasy he inhabited was no doubt pleasant to him. No one understood his moods any more except David Drinkwater. He had turned night into day, roaming the parish under the moon with his shot gun, accompanied by two lurcher dogs.

The Jubilee bonfire on Bredon Hill was the work of David Drinkwater, helped by the Squire's men. Uncle Jim and Henry Watchet hauled the faggots of wood from the larch plantations and the sally coppices to make the beacon. On the great day the Rev. Harrison held a service here at St. Barbara's, when the men belonging to the Sick and Dividend Club paraded with their brass-mounted staffs to the church. The Cirencester and Tewkesbury Conservative Sick and Dividend Society, to give it its proper name, had been founded by Mr. Packer in 1876, and became a godsend to the poorly paid man on the land in time of illness. Sick and Dividend meant exactly what it says. Money for the sick, dividend at the end of the year.

Uncle Jim has told me his recollections of the Jubilee so many times that I feel as if I've been there myself with those celebrating Victorians. Union Jacks were waving from the village cross and outside the Star Inn. William Archer was presented with two Jubilee plates by David Drinkwater, as were all the other families in the village. The Alderton Brass Band came here after the big dinner in the Manor barn and played up and down the village street. The Sedgeberrow men came with their guns and challenged the Ashton marksmen at sparrow shooting in Townsend Close. Tom Archer, my dad, was eleven, and he and the other boys and girls raced for pennies, then had tea and ate blancmange and cake on the Squire's lawn.

The Squire had been hiding himself away for two months, but he did come out that day and joined in the festivities, a sad figure drifting amid the celebrations.

"Keeping you busy, Jim boy," he said to Jim, as Uncle was carrying two buckets of cider from the cider house to the field; buckets swinging from the yokes across his shoulders.

"Yes, sir," Jim replied, "it's thirsty work today."

"Remember, boy, when I stopped you drinking at the show in my meadow, Ten Furlongs, a few years back?"

Jim remembered the Squire shouting, "Stand back, young fella. You're not old enough," when Uncle took his tot to the barrel when the horse race was on. But that had been many years ago, not a few, and now

Uncle Jim, with Henry Watchet, were two of the very few able-bodied men on the farm.

As always, when a man's mind ceases to act rationally and that man has been a benefactor to all and sundry, some folk take advantage. Men stole his crops. They charged him excess for the things he bought for the house and the farm. They poached his game.

The men in his fields were men who used to be able to carry a two hundredweight and a quarter sack of wheat up the granary steps. Now they were about able to carry the empty sack. But he paid them the same money as Jim Archer and Henry Watchet. When threshing time came Uncle Jim said it was a sight for sore eyes. Men hobbling on sticks, trying to carry the chaff and stack the straw. Seven men were needed to run the machine smoothly, but the Squire was obliged to employ eleven.

When Uncle and Henry had finished four days' carrying the sacks of corn up the steps into the granary, Uncle Jim asked the Squire for more wages. "You are getting the same as the others, boy, eleven shillings a week, and drinking plenty of my best cider and eating boiled bacon and cheese for Sunday breakfast in my kitchen for working on Sunday with the cows. No, Jim, no more money for you, but I've a suggestion."

"What's that, sir?" Uncle said.

The Squire put his hand into his leather purse and showed Jim one hundred golden sovereigns. "Here's one hundred of these if you will do a job for me."

Uncle was nonplussed, never having seen so much money in his life before. The Squire left him for a

208

minute and came back carrying his gun and a box of cartridges. "Here's the gun, Jim, and the cartridges, and the one hundred sovereigns are yours if you will go and shoot the doctor up the road. He's offended me."

"But they 'ull hang me, sir, for that," Uncle replied.

The Squire looked at the young man and said quietly, "With one hundred sovereigns you can go to America. I might go there myself one day."

The morning was cold and frosty, the moat pond at the back of the Manor was alive with boys from school sliding from the churchyard wall to the hawthorns at the other edge, past the little island where the moorhens nested.

The Squire walked with Jim Archer to the cider house in the orchard below, beside him his two lurcher dogs, a couple of terriers at his heels, and a rough-looking collie in attendance. "These dogs are starved to death with cold this morning, Jim, let's give them some cider."

Uncle Jim was dubious about this operation, knowing as he did that the Squire's dogs could be savage. But from a hogshead barrel he filled his costrel cider barrel with a gallon of cider. The men were allowed a gallon a day for threshing. He then took a cider horn which held about a quarter of a pint and filled that. Catching the first terrier he started to pour the amber liquid down the dog's throat; some was going down the throat, while some was spilling on the ground. All the dogs were given cider except one and that was Brindy, one of the lurchers.

"What about Brindy?" the Squire called to Uncle. "You frightened of him, ah?"

Uncle Jim said, "I be, sir, and it's taking all my allowance of cider."

"Tonight's a full moon," said the Squire, flitting off on to a new subject. "I'll want you and Henry Watchet to come up on Bredon with me to shoot some owls. Supper at my house after if you are good fellows and behave yourselves."

The moon shone so clear that winter night that the outline of the summit of the Hill at Great Hill Barn was clearly visible from Grandfather's house. The Squire announced his arrival to collect Uncle Jim by firing off his gun outside at seven o'clock and quite frightening Grandmother and my dad.

So the owl shooting party set off and every time a bird fluttered in the clinging ivy on a hedgerow elm, the Squire levelled his gun and shot. "Fetch it, Jim, and you, Henry," he told the men.

Uncle then had to search with Henry for a bird which the Squire imagined he had shot. He did however shoot a couple of partridges as they were down for the night in the furrow between two steep lands on the Leasows.

In the Manor kitchen afterwards, the Squire had a long galvanised bath placed on a table. Then, after the housekeeper had provided food and drink for her master and the two young men, the Squire lit a lantern and took his shooting companions to the thatched duck pen in the orchard. "Hold the lantern, boy," he said to Uncle.

He then caught four drakes, resplendent in their green and black head-dress, and carried them under his arms back to the kitchen.

"Are you going to kill them, sir?" Henry said.

"Wait and see," he replied. "You hold two and Jim hold the other two."

Squire Baldwyn then took several bottles of port and poured the port into the bath. Next, one by one, he put the drakes into it, laughing as they swam around. "Now for the sport," he exclaimed, as he marked one drake with red raddle, another with blue, the third with some yellow ochre, and left the fourth unmarked. From his pocket he took a handful of pennies, giving an equal amount to Jim and Henry and keeping the same amount for himself. The pennies were placed in piles on the kitchen table. Placing pieces of soaked bread at one end of the bath, floating on the port, the Squire and Uncle and Henry held the drakes at the other, betting on which one would swim first to the end where the bread was.

"Your win, Henry, on the blue," he called and Jim and the Squire each gave a penny and put it on Henry's pile.

This game went on until the drakes had each gobbled enough bread to satisfy them and just swam around the bath fully satisfied. When the drakes had been returned to the duck pen Squire William took three mugs off the kitchen dresser and ladled out the port bath between them. It was a befuddled pair of Ashton men who walked the wheel-rutted lane to their homes that night. "And didn't your grandmother tell

211

me my fortune when I got home," Uncle recalled to me.

By 1893 both the Squire and Grandfather were feeling their age. The spare, lean, gaitered William Baldwyn developed a stoop. He had given up hunting and was driven around the estate by Joe Salter in a pony and trap. Broad shouldered and stoutish, Grandfather was now a rheumaticky man who suffered with his legs from the foolhardy practice of shin kicking in his youth.

After working some time at the Manor, my dad joined the little bunch of young men from Ashton who made the early morning journey down Gypsies Lane, across the railway crossing, and Carrants Field, by Tinkers Hut and Didcot to Dumbleton to work in the brick yard. The hours were from six in the morning to six at night, knocking off at four o'clock on Saturdays. The steam whistle blew at six a.m. and if you weren't at the brickyard by then you lost a quarter of a day's wages. Seventy hours a week for eighteen shillings, wheeling heavy loads of wet bricks from the pug mill to the kiln. Dad described the narrow planked way along which they had to steer the heavy barrow loads. The bricks, stacked in layers, were difficult to wheel when the clay was on the wet side, for they would slip on the barrow. Ding-dong, all day the men worked because when they returned with the empty wheelbarrow to the pug mill, another loaded barrow awaited them. Slavery this was, by today's standards, but the fresh air of the country, the reasonable living on wholesome bread, fresh vegetables, bacon and the odd snared rabbit,

212

made this life infinitely better than the lot of the worker in the smoke of the town.

That year of 1893 many changes took place in the village, for after a hot summer a hard winter followed. The influenza epidemic took off George Archer who had married Alf Stubbs' widow, then Martha Dunn died and Fred Dunn went to the Evesham Infirmary. Spider Watchet, who had been clerk and sexton since the time of the Archdeacon, was helped now by his son, Henry, as gravedigger. Walter and Fanny Peart seemed an ageless couple. Walter still propelled himself up Bredon Hill with his crook, now that the Squire had bought a bunch of fifty ewes at Beckford market expressly for the old man to tend.

The Squire had had a rick of wheat built on staddle stones in Jubilee year, 1887. He declared to David Drinkwater that the rick would not be threshed until the old Queen had a Diamond Jubilee.

"She may not live that long," David said.

"Them as lives longest 'ull see the most," the Squire replied.

In 1897 the Queen did celebrate her Diamond Jubilee. The rick at the Manor had been rethatched every year and Joe Salter put ferrets in loose to move any rats that may have defied the mushroom tops of the staddle stones.

Joe drove the old Squire down to Carrants Field to ask William Archer if he would leave his land for a couple of days and help with the threshing. "Not much of a man now, sir," Grandfather said.

"Better than some as come to me and work in a fashion," the Squire replied.

So Grandfather came to the Manor that winter morning to build a load of straw on to a farm waggon, for it was second nature to William Archer to stack the tied boltings of straw on a waggon or to build a rick.

The dust that day was unbelievable, Uncle Jim said. In ten years the sheaves had become dusty through the mice which had entered the rick. The load was nearly on the waggon. Long Fred pitched the boltings up to Grandfather. Then tragedy occurred. The fore ladder of the waggon, that is, the wooden front rave which holds up the front of the load, snapped, and Grandfather fell, hitting his head on the stone floor of the rickyard. He lay there unconscious and the men didn't know what to do. But in those days men were expected to be tougher than the horses they worked with, the survival of the fittest being a reality. So Grandfather was lifted up on to a bed of straw in a muck cart, while Joe Salter led the horse which took him unconscious up the village lane, his head bouncing unsupported on the straw as the cart passed over cobbles and wheel ruts. Uncle Jim carried him up the stairs into bed while Grandmother sent Polly for the doctor.

Our doctor could do little for an old man with a fractured skull, but said that ice from the fishmongers would help him. Propped between the pillows Grandfather lay, while Grandmother waited for Dad to come back from Evesham where he had gone to fetch the ice.

After a few weeks in a state of unconsciousness and then a few more semi-conscious, Grandfather was able to get about once more and eventually he would hobble down to Carrants Field again to work when he felt like it. The rhubarb and parsnip wine had a dulling effect on his memory and seemed to divorce him from the realities of old age and infirmity. But his health was broken, never to recover completely.

Uncle Jim and Dad worked all the hours they could spare to keep the land cultivated, planted, and the crops harvested. William Archer was now a kind of sleeping partner in a little enterprise which had been his life for more than fifty years. No pension, no compensation, but a little help from the Cirencester and Tewkesbury Conservative Sick and Dividend Society. Luckily Mary Ann still had money in the stocking and with the produce of the land and help from the family, they survived. It was unthinkable for them to accept Parish Relief, for being beholden to the Parish was frowned upon in the 1890s.

Grandfather walked with an ash plant stick now, but he still drove a donkey cart up and down the lane, bringing home his potatoes and other vegetables in season. He loved the half dozen tabby cats around the stables and his tree-shaded garden. And now there was a Baptist Chapel in the village, which he attended every Sunday at six with Mary Ann. But old William Archer in the evening of his life became what Uncle Jim described as "stomach full", a stubborn, difficult man. He once treated a neighbour who tried to shelter from the rain in his hovel uninvited to a punch in the mouth and he had become a man who could not stand impudence from boys and girls in the village and he didn't suffer fools gladly. Joe Salter had married and had two sons. The younger boy Uncle Jim called "a gallus lad", up to devilment. He, with others, practised the age-old trick of dangling a button on a cotton thread outside a window, then, from a safe distance, pulling the reel of cotton and causing the button to rattle on the window pane. The boy had annoyed William for several winter nights with the cotton and button nuisance. In the village one day William called to young Salter, "Here, boy, I owe you a penny." The boy went to him expecting the money, but William swung his stick and rapped him across the shoulders. "There," he said, "just keep away from my window, there's a good lad."

Uncle Jim's description of Grandfather in his old age conjures up the picture of a man whose land at Carrants Field had given some independence. Carrants Field, though small, was his estate, and as the Squire ruled the Manor, so Grandfather was the ruler of Carrants Field.

Dad was now deeply involved as a soldier in the relatively new Salvation Army. He practised the euphonium in the stable at the top of William's garden. He cycled to Evesham on Sundays to the meetings, spoke to the crowds in the Saturday market place, collected for self-denial, and met General Booth, whom he almost worshipped, at Cheltenham.

In those days of no music in the home except the Sunday evenings around a cottage piano or harmonium, the music of the Salvation Army Band was, to put it in modern terms, "Top of the Pops" on those Saturday nights in the crowded market place. When Dad became proficient playing his euphonium he did solos in Evesham Town Hall at Salvation Army Rallies. He played favourite hymns at home to Mary Ann and old William, who asked time and time again for what he called old Methody tunes. "Play the one, Tom, we used to sing at Merecombe," he'd say.

Dad bought a phonograph at a sale with two hampers full of cylinder records. William Archer in his last days, marvelled at the voices from the wax "records". To him, who couldn't read, the phonograph acted as a balm to the man whose life had been so close to the soil.

At the Manor, Squire Baldwyn had employed one bailiff after another. They all robbed him by selling pigs and horses to dealers and keeping the money. Eventually the Squire appointed a cousin to manage the farm, an honest, thrifty young man who did his best to pull things together, though the Squire still insisted on keeping the great number of unbroken horses on Bredon Hill. And he still remembered Fly By Night. "He would have won me thousands of pounds if the going had not been so hard," the Squire was wont to say.

When William Baldwyn became so trigger happy with his gun, shooting up the chimneys of the Manor at imaginary owls and scaring the daylights out of his housekeeper, his cousin who managed the farm arranged for a male nurse to look after him and for him to be securely locked in his room at night and for the shot to be taken from his cartridges.

Joe Salter still took the master of the Manor around during the day, but now accompanied by the male nurse. He would sit in the pony trap on the headland while Long Fred and Spider Watchet's boy, Henry, ploughed the Beckfords Way with the steam traction engine, and Long Fred would blow the steam whistle to amuse his old master.

On wet days Joe Salter drove him to the village school for the old Squire to pick out three or four of the bigger boys to come to the farm and clean the brasses of his engines.

"Ah," he said to his carter when he ungeared the plough horses, "I'll bet you haven't ploughed more than an acre today on the Hill and Long Fred has ploughed six acres along Beckfords Way."

"Yes, Squire," the carter replied, "but my team can keep going when the wet weather comes, but Long Fred's engines won't."

Once again Uncle Jim asked the Squire for a rise in his wages and when he was once again refused, Uncle left the Manor and went off to seek his fortune in Leicestershire.

The following summer the Squire had been around the farm buildings feeding the fowls, as was his practice, when Jim Dance and the nurse missed him for a while. David Drinkwater was in the yard and he joined in the search. "Perhaps he's gone to see the ducks on the moat pond," he suggested.

David walked past the Tythe Barn to the moat pond near St. Barbara's church. The ducks and drakes were quacking loudly near the bank under the hawthorn. In the middle of the shallow pond David spotted a little old man in breeches sitting in a wheelbarrow.

"William, what are you doing?" David Drinkwater called and he waded to the middle of the pond, pulling William Baldwyn and the wheelbarrow to the bank.

"I'm sick to death of this country, David, I'm going to sail to America," was the unexpected reply from Squire Baldwyn.

"In a wheelbarrow," David said.

"Yes, in a wheelbarrow because I'm too miserable to live and too wicked to die."

"Come with me and let's crack a bottle of wine in your room by the fire, William, for old times sake."

They met Joe Salter and the nurse on their way to the Manor. The nurse found some dry clothes for the Squire and left the two men together. David Drinkwater had been a true friend for life to Squire Baldwyn. He was too upright a man to stoop to obtain money off this eccentric, yet good natured old gentleman. David's father, his grandfather, and all the Drinkwaters before, had a name which was never smeared by deceit. As the Squire sat and drank wine with David Drinkwater, they talked of happier days when they were young in the hunting field and at the pheasant shoots. The Rev. Joseph Harrison joined them when he had heard of the moat incident. He rode his horse from Beckford and stabled it with Joe Salter.

"How are you, my friend?" the Vicar asked sympathetically.

"Too miserable to live and too wicked to die, Joseph," was the reply.

The Vicar sat and drank and the three men lit the churchwarden pipes after filling them from the tobacco bowl. The log fire back in the ingle burned brightly. The warmth from it made the Vicar sleepy. When he had nodded off, the Squire said to David with a smile, "His Reverence wasn't exactly dry when he came here. I dare say he's been drinking William Archer's parsnip wine."

A knock came at the door. It was Joe Salter. "The coalman's come to see you from Beckford, sir," he said.

"Do you want any more coal, Master Baldwyn?" the little man with the coal-black face enquired.

"More coal, coalman. Ah, no, I don't. We had to burn the last lot you brought us."

Joe Salter and David Drinkwater had to laugh at that answer, but whether the Squire's humour was unconscious or not they never knew.

The following day Joe Salter and the nurse drove Squire Baldwyn along the Beckford Way to watch Long Fred ploughing with what the Squire called his black horses. As the pony and trap passed the ash tree where the culvert comes under the road, carrying the water from Paris Springs to the Carrants Brook, the old Squire fell forward and his life ended like a snuffed candle.

So the end came to a flamboyant character who had been at the centre of a village lying under Bredon Hill.

Squire William, being a bachelor, was the last of the Baldwyn squires who for five hundred years had scratched the top few inches of soil, reared and fattened sheep and cattle and supported the Church.

Some months later, Grandfather Archer was in Carrants Field with Mary Ann, dropping seed potatoes in the furrows Dad had ploughed out with a couple of David Drinkwater's horses. They rode together back to the house and stabled the donkey. Grandfather William wound up the clock at nine, as was his custom, and they all went to bed.

"I think I'll lie in for an hour this morning, Tom," he said to Dad the next morning.

Grandmother got breakfast, then went back upstairs. It was quiet up there and she placed her hand on William's brow. He didn't move. He had died in his sleep on April 13th 1900, just a week before the cuckoo would come to his pear tree in the garden, a month before the elm leaves would show pale green in the hedgerow at the back under Bredon Hill telling him it would soon be time for planting runner beans in Carrants Field.

Millie Watchet laid the old man out and the doctor, when he called, enquired about the marks of buttons on his shins. "Poor boy," Mary Ann cried as the doctor unclasped the belt Grandfather had won for the champion shin kicker of Bredon Hill. "Those are the marks of his gaiter buttons, Doctor. He suffered with his legs from the folly of his youth."

By the church porch he lies, the remains of a man who soldiered on from his birth in George IV's reign, right through the Victorian period. We will never again see the like of men such as Grandfather William and his brothers, or of Alf Stubbs, Sam Tombs, Walter Peart, Long Fred and Spider Watchet. Such men are best described by some verses of Edmund Blunden from his poem called "Forefathers".

> Here they went with smock and crook,
>   Toiled in the sun, lolled in the shade,
> Here they mudded out the brook
>   And here their hatchet cleared the glade:
> Harvest-supper woke their wit,
> Huntsman's moon their wooings lit.
>
> From this church they led their brides,
>   From this church themselves were led
> Shoulder-high; on these waysides
>   Sat to take their beer and bread.
> Names are gone — what men they were
> These their cottages declare.
>
> Names are vanished, save the few
>   In the old brown Bible scrawled;
> These were men of pith and thew,
>   Whom the city never called;
> Scarce could read or hold a quill
> Built the barn, the forge, the mill.
>
> Unrecorded, unrenowned,
>   Men from whom my ways begin.